HOW to Say NO

Michelle Elman

ILLUSTRATED BY SARA TOMATE

How to Say NO

PUFFIN

PUFFIN BOOKS

UK | USA | Canada | Ireland | Australia
India | New Zealand | South Africa

Puffin Books is part of the Penguin Random House group of companies
whose addresses can be found at global.penguinrandomhouse.com

www.penguin.co.uk
www.puffin.co.uk
www.ladybird.co.uk

Penguin
Random House
UK

First published 2023

001

Printed and bound in Spain

The authorized representative in the EEA is Penguin Random House
Ireland, Morrison Chambers, 32 Nassau Street, Dublin D02 YH68

A CIP catalogue record for this book is available from the British Library

ISBN: 978–0–241–63409–7

All correspondence to:
Puffin Books
Penguin Random House Children's
One Embassy Gardens, 8 Viaduct Gardens, London SW11 7BW

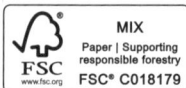

To Rafferty, Boaz and Zahara –
may your no always be
as strong as your yes!

Contents

Introduction

No is your new best friend!

Being a young person is not easy. If you ask most adults if they would return to adolescence, it would be a no: a firm no, a *hell no*. And the worst part is . . . 'no' is the word you never seem to be allowed to use!

There were so many times growing up when I wished I could shout 'NO' from the rooftops:

- When the other girls in my primary school class and I were made to undress in front of the boys for PE.

- When my brother would come barging into my room when I just wanted to be left alone, and then I'd get told off for locking the door.

- When my friends tried to pressure me into doing something that made me feel uncomfortable but I didn't want to seem uncool.

- When I was told to do things that felt unfair, and heard 'you're too young to understand' or 'because I say so' when I questioned it.

Hearing those phrases still makes my eyes roll. I mean, it just doesn't make sense! At your age, you have intelligence, smarts and opinions, and yet none of the autonomy.

Autonomy: The quality of being independent, free and self-directing.

That's what you want, right? You don't just want to be an actor in your own life – you want to be the director! If you are the actor, you have to listen when they call 'NO PHONES ON SET', but if you are the director, you can make your own phone rules. If you are the actor, you get told what to do with your body and where to go. Be the director, though, and you get to change the directions. Your life should be YOUR movie, YOUR set and YOUR choice!

As a young person, you are a free-thinking individual without any of the freedom that comes with adulthood. Your choices are limited and you rarely have control over them. You don't get to decide where you live, you may not get much choice which school you go to, and you might not even get to decide what you're having for dinner! Everyone seems to want to dismiss your opinions because you 'are too young to get it'. Patronizing, much? You know what you think and feel, yet you are also constantly told that 'you're only a child'. It's frustrating and can make you feel helpless, hopeless and powerless. It seems like everyone is always telling you 'no', but you use the word yourself, and suddenly heads roll. What's fair about that?!

Fast-forward a few years, and suddenly you're catapulted from school (where you need to do exactly as you are told) to adulthood, where you're meant to know exactly who you are, what you want to do and what you believe in. So at some point, the rules change and NO ONE explains the new ones! Except that the rules don't change overnight – they start to happen in a murky, blurry, complicated period, otherwise known as growing up.

These are the years that are most difficult to navigate. Growing up is a minefield. You have to navigate new friendships, new teachers, body changes, there never seem to be enough hours in the day, people are kissing, and suddenly everyone is posting their breakfast on social media?! If you've picked up this book, I'm assuming you are stuck in these years, so I want to say first of all that you are doing the best you can, and second of all that **you deserve to say 'no'**. In fact, I'm here to give you an all-access pass to the word **NO**. (And if you are a parent or teacher reading this, then I pinky promise I will talk about when it's OK and appropriate to say no and also about listening when other people tell you no, so don't worry!)

It took me many years to find my voice and what I now realize is that I always had the power to say no, but when I used this power as a kid I was labelled as '**difficult**' and '**stubborn**'. But what's wrong with knowing what you do and don't want? The moment you start using the word 'no', you are gaining control! You don't need to be a people-pleaser. You don't need to say yes to get people to like you more. Saying no will not make you lose the people who love you.

And if someone tells you otherwise? Well that's a

big, bold-faced LIE.

You are allowed to say no.

The key to unlocking your power is to be able to use this two-letter word in the **right way** – in a way that is firm, confident and reasonable. If you can't use the word 'no' properly, then not only is it really hard to let others know what you think and feel, but **your 'yes' has less power too**.

Be honest with yourself. Why are you actually saying YES?

yes

to the party because you want to go, **OR**

yes

to the party because you don't want to be left out?

YES

to the phone call because you want to talk, **OR**

Yes

to the phone call because you don't want to hurt someone's feelings?

6

YES

to a hug because you want a hug, **OR**

YES

to a hug because you don't want to be rude?

When I was a teenager, I cared so much about people liking me, and so I found myself saying yes a lot. But what made it even harder was that I didn't like myself very much. I thought I was ugly, uncool and unpopular, and so I tried to get people to like me by being 'useful'. If they wanted someone to help them with their homework, I was there. If people were mean to me, I didn't mind (I would just cry later!) and if I wasn't invited somewhere, that was fine – I'd claim I didn't want to go anyway. I thought this was the solution to having more friends, but actually it meant I never treated myself well, and neither did anyone else.

But then I discovered boundaries.

Boundaries are simply the way we teach the world how to treat us. If you let people walk all over you, they will. This won't make people like or respect you more, it will only make you feel worse about yourself.

Boundaries are the lines between who we are and who the world wants us to be.

Boundaries are like an invisible shield that keeps you protected. You can lower the shield once you know someone is safe, trustworthy and one of the good ones . . . and you can put it up if someone is being nasty! It's like the block button on your phone, except boundaries are your block button in real life.

Boundaries are how we teach the world what is and isn't acceptable to us, and in order to say what is not acceptable, **we have to be able to use the word 'no'**. 'No' is the first boundary we learn, and the most important! 'No' is my favourite word, even though I know we've always been told that 'yes' is the fun word.

Yes to parties!
  Yes to cake!
    Yes to holidays!

But 'no' is the one that holds all the power. 'No' makes you strong. 'No' makes you confident – I promise. And once you start saying 'no', you won't want to stop.

'No, that is not OK.'
    'No, I do not deserve that.'
    'No, you can't speak to me like that.'

No to bullies!
  No to frenemies!
    No to caring what people think!

I didn't learn to say it properly until I was an adult. I might as well have worn a sign that said 'walk all over me' when I was a child. And the adults in my life were no help either – they couldn't even set their own boundaries! So I learned them the hard way – through a lot of tears and heartache. I hope this book provides you with all the tools I wish I'd had, to save you the unnecessary pain of keeping people around who treat you like rubbish and make you do things you don't want to do!

And the trick is, we all need to embrace our inner toddler a bit more. The toddler who would yell 'no' when their toy was stolen or cry when put into the arms of a weird stranger. We get the toddler taken out of us over time, as we get taught to ignore our own discomfort and prioritize everyone else out of politeness and ease. We unlearn that we deserve to say 'no' when our friends want us to do something we don't want to do. We unlearn our right to say 'no' when people invade our personal space. We unlearn that we can say 'no' and put our foot down sometimes.

In this book, I'm going to teach you how to take the vibes of a toddler, mix in the language of an adult and set your own boundaries.

And it all starts with NO.

Do you need to say 'no' more?

Are you a person with good boundaries, or are you someone who needs to build up their 'no' muscle? Let's find out!

Do you use these phrases a lot?

'No worries if not!'
. . . when you are worried.

'I don't mind'
. . . when you do mind.

'I don't care'
. . . when you definitely care.

'It's not that bad'
. . . when it is that bad.

'I can handle it'
. . . when you can't handle it.

'It's fine'
. . . when it's not fine.

'It doesn't matter'
. . . when it does matter.

'Forget about it'
. . . when you shouldn't forget about it.

Now we need to look at the words you use to describe yourself!

Do you ever think that you are ...

A bother?
A nuisance?
In everyone's way?

If you think this way, then of course you are going to feel the pressure to please people! When we care too much about making everyone else around us happy, it's often because we don't feel good enough in our own skin, so we work extra hard to be easy to be around. We try to act perfectly so that we aren't annoying, but the problem is that if we care too much about what others think, then we aren't thinking about ourselves enough!

And our most important job is to make sure we are OK too!

Chapter 1
Saying
no to
friends

- What if I don't go to a party and they stop inviting me forever?

- What if I say 'no' and then regret it later?

- What if they hate me if I don't do what they want?

- Doesn't being a good friend mean *always* being there for them?

- Do all my friends secretly hate me?

- What if they think I'm boring for not telling them secrets?

Friends are sometimes the hardest people to say no to – you want to be liked, you want to seem fun and you don't want to miss out on being invited to parties! But you can have enjoyable and healthy relationships with your friends while still making time for yourself and knowing when to say no. You shouldn't have to forget your needs in order to make your friends happy! Friendships should be equal, and friends should like you for who you are. If a friend keeps making you feel uncomfortable and crossing your boundaries, it might be time to question whether they're a good friend to have in your life at all . . .

I am not the Sun; I can't be the centre of your universe

When I was younger, I worried a lot about losing all my friends and I would do anything to not let that happen. This is when all the people-pleasing started. I thought if I became a really, really good friend, then they'd have to keep me around whether they liked me or not! If my friends asked me to do *anything*, I would drop what I was doing and be there for them in an instant. I remember asking my mum to sign me up for roller hockey lessons even though I hated it, simply because my best friend asked me to. She loved roller hockey and didn't want to be alone, so even though it made my back hurt and I didn't like rollerblading or hockey, I said yes when I wanted to say no. And since I was awful at it, I got a lot of bruises to show for it! But at least I was being a good friend, right? So what was the problem?

The problem was a lot of the things I was doing were coming at the expense of myself. I was already doing tennis, swimming, ice-skating and horse-riding, and adding roller hockey to the list meant I never had a free afternoon after school and I would end up doing my homework late into the evening. I was exhausted, but I put all my energy into being 'a good friend' because my fear of losing friends was so great.

It's important to be a good friend, but this shouldn't compromise you being able to look after yourself.

Being willing to do **anything** for your friends is actually not healthy. You should never be someone who bends over backwards for your friends, and this type of behaviour can sometimes harm rather than help your friendships. For example, one way I tried to be liked was by being the person with all the gossip. I would always be the go-to person who people would tell their secrets to, and when I was worried that I wouldn't be included, I would spill these secrets so that my supposed friends would keep me around. Then one day I turned up to school with the reputation that I was a gossip, and I **hated** that! It was an awful way to make friends and I always felt like I was at risk of losing my spot in the group if I didn't deliver enough news, or if the news I had wasn't quite juicy enough. What's worse was that even though I tried to be a really, really good friend, actually being a gossip made me untrustworthy and quite a bad friend.

What I know now is that if the only reason your friends are keeping you around is that you always have the best gossip, or because you will drop everything for them, that's actually not friendship. Of course we want our friends to like us, but we want them to like us because of **who we are**, not because of **what we do for them**. Friendship is about supporting each other, but true friends want you to take care of yourself as well. And if you have to convince someone to be friends with you, then that's not a friend you want.

So how can you make sure you aren't becoming the centre of someone else's universe?

You don't have to be there for every moment in their life. Has one of your friends ever called and before you could even say 'hello', they've blurted out all their problems? Well, this is called an **emotional dump**. Imagine each emotion as a heavy book, and they've taken a whole stack and gone **PLONK** in your lap. **OUCH**. What your friend should have done is to ask first. That is good boundaries . . .

'Hey! I had an awful day; can I talk to you about it?'

And you can say **no**!

'So sorry to hear that! That sucks! I'm actually out at the moment. Can we talk about it tomorrow?'

Or:

'Oh no! I've had a rubbish day too so was going to go to sleep early. Do you have someone else you can talk to?'

Real friendship is saying, 'I will support you as long as I'm OK too'. As they say on aeroplanes, put your own oxygen mask on before helping anyone else. In other words, if you don't help yourself first, you are no help to the people around you.

But doesn't that make me a bad person?

No! You are not being a bad friend by saying no. You are not being mean. You are not being selfish. There is only one you in the world and you need to look after yourself – that should always be your top priority!

You don't need to feel your friend's feelings, either. Has your friend ever been so angry that you've become angry for them? It's easy to absorb the emotions of other people, but it's important to learn how to have empathy without taking on someone else's pain. Having good boundaries means being able to know the difference between emotions that are happening in your own body and the emotions happening in someone else's.

When you carry your friend's emotions for them, it's like carrying two backpacks. You've already got your own, so now you're going to feel exhausted carrying both, and your friend will never learn how to carry theirs. Instead, you could support your friend by cheering them on, or showing them how to adjust the straps – this way, both of you can manage your own load. Emotions work the same: you can show support and love for your friend without taking on their emotions yourself.

If I'm a friend to you, then you need to be a friend to me too!

We want friendships in our life that are equal. Someone who is kind both to your face and behind your back. Someone who listens to you when you talk and doesn't just expect you to listen to them. But if you have a friend who doesn't treat you equally right now, that doesn't mean the friendship needs to be over. A key part of having boundaries is noticing something that you don't like and saying something about it.

'I don't like that you ignore me at school and only want to talk to me when we are on the bus home.'

'It's not nice that you treat me differently when certain people are around.'

'I heard you told the whole class the secret I told you. It really upset me, and it has broken my trust.'

If they respond well and you see them changing their behaviour, that's a sign of a good friend. As long as people are willing to change, that's all you can ask of them. Remember, no one is perfect, and *you* might be doing things that upset people without even realizing . . .

Good friends accept when they are wrong!

So, what if someone is hurt by something you have done? Well . . . if you want people to take your emotions seriously, then you have to take other people's emotions seriously too. Apologies are important and we have to be very deliberate with the word 'sorry'.

Sometimes people overuse the word by sprinkling it everywhere. They might even say sorry to a door when they walk into it! And some people **NEVER** use it, even if they know they are wrong. You need to find somewhere in the middle. Saying 'sorry' is a way to make things right when you know you've done wrong. And if you are too angry right now to admit you are wrong, take some time to cool off – but that word needs to be said!

You don't have to go to every party!

When we get invited somewhere, or get asked to do something, our knee-jerk reaction is often just to say yes. After all, we should be grateful they are asking us, right? And we wouldn't want to risk them not asking us in the future by saying no, would we? And maybe we might actually feel like it on the day . . .

Wrong wrong wrong!

Why do we often say yes to things we don't want to do?

- **We are worried that they will be angry or upset if we don't.**
  If you say no to that sleepover, of course your friends might be sad not to have you there, but they will respect your reason for not going. And they will still enjoy the sleepover without you!

- **We are worried they won't ask again.**
  It feels good to be included, so it can feel scary to say no and risk losing your invite forever. But saying no this time doesn't mean there won't be a next time; your friends won't suddenly stop inviting you to things.

- **We need a reason to say no.**
  Not wanting to go is a big enough reason! When you get an invite or a request to do something, just pause and ask yourself: 'Do I want to?' If the answer is no, then that's OK!

There is a right and wrong way to say no. The difference comes down to timing and your reason. First, it's best to say no as soon as possible if you don't want to go, as it can be hurtful if someone lets you down at the last minute. And second, your reason should be honest. You don't need to lie about a family event – they'll probably know you're lying! It's best to just tell the truth so they know you aren't saying no to being friends, you are just saying no to that one event.

You are still lovable even if you don't have a best friend!

Before we move on, I want to talk to you about the idea of a 'best friend'. Now, I know sometimes it can seem like everyone in the world has a ride-or-die BFF. In every movie, there is a best friend, and if you didn't meet yours the moment you walked into nursery, then you might begin to feel unlovable or not good enough in some way. I have news for you! This is NOT true. In fact, having one friend be your everything isn't always a good thing.

We can't rely on one person for all our needs. Think about your friendships like a garden: some plants grow better in cold weather, some prefer lots of sun and others love the rain. If you plant all these different types, then your garden will grow all year round. In the same way, if you have different friends you can go to for different things, your life will likely be healthy, full and balanced.

Have a think about the various things you love to do with friends. Then grab a pen and paper and write down a *different* name beside each activity. You could fill in the names of friends, siblings, relatives or even a '?' if you haven't found that person yet who you can do that activity with. There's no shame in that at all! This way, you can make sure you have different people for different occasions, and this will stop you relying too heavily on just one person. Because remember – no one should be the centre of *anyone* else's universe!

Here are some examples:

- **A friend who you love sleepovers with**

- **Someone whose family you feel really close to**

- **A person who you have all your best DMCs (Deep Meaningful Conversations) with**

- **A friend who you share a hobby with**

- **Someone who you study with**

Remember, friendships are not a competition. You're allowed to have multiple friends and your friends have the same right too! Just because your friend is close to one person, it doesn't mean they are any less close to you. You can have two friends you are equally close to, and you don't have to choose one over the other! I wish I'd realized at school that being in a group of three didn't mean competing for the top best-friend spot. Instead, it was wonderful that we had two people to go to when we were down and two people to cheer us on when we were winning. **The more the merrier!**

Having more people in your life is never a bad thing. We all need a support network. In this network, you can have new friends who you aren't ready to share all your secrets with yet, and you can have old friends who you only want to see once in a while. You do not have to give all your friends the same access to your life and information. And if there are some things you want to keep secret, that's a good thing – it just means you have strong boundaries!

I am perfect exactly as I am

Is there a kid at your school who is just effortlessly cool, who doesn't seem to care whether people like them or not? How do they do it? It seems that even when people dislike them, they keep being themselves. And that's the trick! They don't change themselves for anyone.

There are eight billion people in the world, and someone, somewhere is going to dislike you. And that's OK. Can you imagine how exhausting it would be to try to get all eight billion people to like you?

And sometimes there will be people who dislike you who barely even know you! I'll admit to you that I've sometimes decided I don't like a celebrity, for no particular reason. I don't know them at all, and yet I don't like them. How is that fair? Well ... it's not. But it happens. We all make up our minds about people way too quickly – sometimes we decide we don't like someone before we know them, and sometimes we decide we *really* like someone and want to be their friend. And something we all need to remember is that people change their minds **all the time!** I mean, we all know someone we once disliked and then, when we actually spoke to them properly, realized they weren't that bad!

Now, why am I telling you all this? And what does this have to do with setting rules and boundaries for your life? The key lesson I want you to take away is that **other people's opinions don't matter.**

What actually is an opinion?

Opinion: A view or judgement formed about something, not necessarily based on fact or knowledge.

Did you hear that? An opinion is not a fact! It can be based on complete nonsense. And are you going to let complete nonsense ruin your life? **Hell, no!**

One of the best boundaries I have ever set is the following golden rule: **It is not my job to change people's minds about me.** In other words, if I sense that someone dislikes me or has certain opinions about me, instead of trying to change that, I now say: 'You are allowed to think that!' If they don't like you and you allow yourself not to care, then it won't affect you. It's as simple as that.

When you take in someone else's opinion and change yourself for them, what you are telling yourself is that they are right and you are wrong. You are telling yourself that they know better than you do about who you are and who you should be. And that's just not true! If you think something is cool and someone else doesn't, who says they are right? If you think something is fun and they find it boring, can't both be true?

For example, take a look at some of my opinions . . .

● **Soy sauce is the best condiment on eggs!**

● **Pineapple on pizza is disgusting!**

● **Sleeping naked is way better than pyjamas . . . until there is a fire alarm!**

Grab a pen and paper. I want you to make a list of all the things that you find fun and interesting. It can be anything at all. Then I want you to stay loyal to yourself and your opinions. So, if someone tells you that something is boring and it happens to be on your list, stand your ground. Tell the person that you find it fun and that's OK – people are allowed to enjoy different things.

My definition of cool and your definition of cool are allowed to be different. And the same can be said for boundaries, too. You might hate hugs and I might like them. You might love sharing your clothes with friends and I might not want to share mine with anyone. Feeling confident in yourself and your opinions will help you to set boundaries and say no to things – even if others are saying yes. You don't need to change for anyone.

There is only one you in the world!

I know it can feel scary to stick out, but I want to encourage you to stand out from the crowd and own it. It's time to say no to peer pressure. You don't have to do what your friends are doing. Right now, it might feel like the last thing you want is to be different, but how boring would it be if we were all the same? When you pretend to be like your friends, you might as well all be photocopies of each other, and we all know an original is better than a photocopy. You need to stand alone to realize your own strengths.

I'm in my thirties, and I thought I would have everything figured out by now, but in many ways, I'm no different to when

I was ten. The only difference between then and now is that life experience has taught me that changing myself to fit in doesn't work. I have learned that if I pretend to be someone I am not, it makes me unhappy. I've learned it's better to be hated for who I am than to be loved for who I am not. And being disliked means you can find your people faster. Don't like me? Great, thanks for letting me know sooner rather than later! If a friend doesn't like you for you, it's better to know now so you don't waste any more time with them.

Do you know what a chameleon is? It's a kind of lizard that blends into the colour of its environment, so if it is sitting on a leaf, it will turn green. If you put it on a tree trunk, it will turn brown. It blends in so as not to be noticed, because it's safer for it if other animals can't see it. And sometimes as humans, we can think the same. We might think that if we don't stand out, that makes our lives easier. But if you change yourself to blend into the room like a chameleon, then in every room you are a

different person. This not only makes it hard for others to like you but, more importantly, it makes it very hard to like yourself. Because it's difficult to know who you truly are!

I want you to focus on all the ways you aren't like everyone else – these are what make you unique!

Can you think of three unique things that make you different?

I am unique because .....

I am unique because .....

I am unique because .....

Own your opinions

True friends will value your opinions, even if they are different to theirs. Here is a list of things I love to say no to:

No to rollercoasters!

No to strawberries!

No to rugby!

Now it's your turn. Let's unleash your no. Have a think about some things that you have been saying yes to, when really you've wanted to say no. What do you pretend to like but actually truly hate? Grab a pen and paper, write them down. Then take a long look at that list and make a promise to yourself: I WILL NOT SAY YES TO THESE THINGS JUST SO PEOPLE WILL LIKE ME!

I am not your doormat!

When I was eleven years old, a friend of mine made fun of me for being a teacher's pet. It hurt a lot. She did it in front of the whole class after I kept putting my hand up to answer the questions. I got every question right and I remember my pride disappearing and suddenly feeling really embarrassed as the whole class stared. I didn't want all the attention on me, and it felt like everyone was waiting for me to burst into tears, so do you know how I responded? I laughed it off! I never told my friend how much her words hurt me. I could've easily said, 'Hey, that wasn't cool. I would never say that to you.' But I wasn't used to setting boundaries, and I felt too nervous to say something. I wish I knew then what I know now – the more boundaries you set, the easier it will become.

How different would your life be if, when someone made fun of you, you called them out on it instead of laughing it off? The first time you say something back, you will be scared, but this is because you are doing something new: you are setting a boundary!

A very smart man called Gabor Maté once said:

'Boundaries are not broken in childhood as much as they are never constructed.'

What that means is, you can't know if your boundaries are broken if you don't have any to begin with. We need to set our boundaries so we know when to stand up for ourselves. You can think of boundaries like little protection bubbles. You can explore the world from within your bubble, with only those you love, trust and care about being allowed inside. The people who you let into your bubble need to be people who will take care of it, and anyone who has plans to burst your bubble must be kept away. Boundaries will keep you safe from the wrong people and will let the right people in. That's why boundaries are like a bubble and not a brick wall. We still want and need to let people into our little circle of safety.

So, let's talk about the people who want to burst your bubble. Sometimes you might come across people who will say mean things. They might try and justify this, by telling you that they're just being honest or a good friend.

- **'Your family are weird. What? I'm just being honest!'**

- **'Your skirt is ugly and if a good friend can't tell you that, who will?'**

- **'You are so loud! Someone needed to tell you because we are all thinking it.'**

This makes NO sense! If what they are saying is unkind and makes you feel bad, that person is not being a friend. Mean people do not deserve to be in your life and they are the kind of people who you should keep out of your bubble. When someone is unkind, you need to say something. But what can you say?

- 'Don't speak to me like that.'

- 'That was rude. It's not OK to treat me like that.'

- 'This is not what friendship looks like to me.'

You can do the same when you hear people being unkind about someone else, too. Instead of joining in, which might feel like the easiest thing to do, try saying, 'That's not cool! They are my friend; don't talk about them that way. We're better than that!'

Sometimes people might disguise mean comments as jokes, which can be harder to respond to. They might argue that they're 'just having a laugh', and if you don't find it funny then that's your problem! But if the 'joke' is at someone's expense - this is bullying. If you find yourself in a situation like this, ask them to explain the 'joke'. It will quickly become obvious that they are making YOU the punchline. You could then say:

'That's not funny! Friends don't make each other the butt of the joke.'

If you've ever learned a foreign language, you'll know that saying the words aloud for the first time can feel strange. And you might worry about getting them wrong. The same can be said for when you are learning your new boundary-setting language. It might feel uncomfortable to begin with. But fear can be a good thing: it means you're being brave and trying something new. And when we embrace our fears, there is no limit to what we can do.

Who are you and what have you done with my people-pleasing friend?

When you start standing up for yourself, it might be a shock to some of your friends. Especially if they are used to you being the one who always says yes! They are expecting the people-pleasing you, but that person doesn't exist anymore.

If they call you out for standing up for yourself, this means that you are setting boundaries effectively. You setting a boundary is inconvenient for them, and so they might say things to try to convince you to change your mind. This is when you have to dig deep and not cave in.

Your

bubble

needs

protecting.

'I am not changing my mind. My answer is still no.'

At first it will be shocking and surprising, but then they will get used to this new you. When you say no, set your boundaries and stand by your decisions more regularly, the people around you will start to realize they can't push you around. You are a changed person!

But what if there are people who don't adjust and who don't like the new you? I want you to look at that person's behaviour as a whole.

- **Are they really a good friend to you?**

- **Does it seem like they won't stick around if you won't do what they want?**

- **Do they respect your no?**

- **Do they care about how you think and feel, and listen to your opinions?**

If they don't respect your boundaries, they don't respect YOU. I know that can be hard to hear, but if you have a friend who doesn't respect you or your no, you need to ask yourself whether that's a friend you want in your life at all.

Losing friends sucks and it's not spoken about often. We always talk about 'friends for life' or 'best friends forever'. Why does no one mention that you can be friends with someone for a year or even five years, and the friendship can come to an end? It could be that you used to know every single thing they were thinking and feeling, and now you just see them across the room in class. You still know their mum's name and that they sleep with a toy dog called Cuddles, but you don't actually speak anymore.

It doesn't mean you are a bad person, and it doesn't mean you did anything wrong. Sometimes people stop being friends with each other because they change – they are in different places and they don't get on like they used to. It doesn't mean you are a bad friend, and it doesn't even mean they were a bad friend either! But if you aren't friends anymore because you had different boundaries and weren't respecting each other, then that's a good thing. It is a valid reason to end a friendship, as the best thing you can do is take care of you and protect yourself.

Boundaries are how we teach the world to treat us, and the ultimate boundary is deciding that someone who doesn't treat you well doesn't deserve to be in your life. You might lose friends over the course of your life and when that happens, I want you to remember that this can be a good thing! It just means you're creating room for someone else to come in and treat you how you want and deserve to be treated.

Ten rules for boundaries with your friends

1. **Be a good friend to others, but also to yourself**

2. **Be honest with your friends**

3. **Set boundaries, even if you lose people as a result**

4. **Friends like you for who you are, not what you do for them**

5. **Friends continue to listen, even when you disagree**

6. **You can have friends for different reasons**

7. **Never change yourself just so others like you**

8. **Friends accept your first 'no'**

9. **Keep mean people outside of your bubble**

10. **You are allowed to end friendships if they make you unhappy**

Chapter 2
Saying
no
online

- I don't want to get social media; do I have to?

- How do I unfollow someone without them getting angry at me?

- What if I don't want to share my location with friends?

- Nobody likes my photos – does that mean no one likes me?

- Why does seeing pictures of myself make me sad?

Within the tiny screens of our phones and computers, there is a whole world to explore. And when it comes to social media, that world comes with a few dangers if we don't have our boundaries in check. I'm not going to sit here and tell you that social media is *all* bad. I had a number of operations as a child, and I used to be really insecure about the scars that came from them. Social media was the first place I felt comfortable opening up about them, before I was even able to talk to my friends about it. Social media is also responsible for me meeting at least ten of the closest friends I have in my life. And social media was the first place I found people who looked like me!

There were mixed-race people like me, people who were fat like me and even people with surgery scars like mine! But, being an influencer, I know the dark side too. I know how mean people can be, and I know how it can feel when people leave you horrible comments. I also know how addictive it can be to sit and stare at a screen all day, scrolling, watching, playing, chatting, refreshing. So I want to talk to you about how to do this safely and with those all-important boundaries in place. There are lots of great things that can come from having a world of communication at our fingertips, but it's important to know how to navigate it safely – and when enough is enough.

I don't care what you had for breakfast!

This section is all about who you allow into your online life. Perhaps you don't yet have social media and this chapter doesn't feel as relevant to you. But this information can be useful at any stage of your life – whether you don't yet have a phone, whether you just signed up for your first social media account or whether you're a total tech pro! There's lots of information here about the online world that might be useful to you in future, so take a seat, put your feet up and stick around – there's a lot to learn! (Please also remember that you have to be a certain age before you can join social media platforms. This may feel frustrating, but it's for your own protection.)

Throughout your life, you're likely to come across many people who you wouldn't necessarily choose to spend your time with. For example, those in your class. You might have lots of friends around you, of course, but there might be others in the class too who you aren't as close to. And when a new kid joins the class, that's a new person in your life who you don't really know at all.

When you meet someone new in real life, you might feel like you should add them to your online life too, if you have social media. Or if someone adds or follows you on social media, you might worry that it's rude to not follow them back. But if you do that with everyone you come across, before you know it, the number of people you follow might be in the hundreds . . . and maybe even the thousands!

Who gets the keys to your social media?

Think of your social media like your home. You wouldn't just give anyone a key to your home, would you? You'd give it to people who you trust and who you know will use it respectfully. You definitely wouldn't give it to someone who you worry would snoop around and tell people about what's in your underwear drawer! And you certainly wouldn't give it to a stranger in the street.

It's really easy to hit follow, especially when you're curious and want to have a peek at someone's life, including their life before you met them. But remember that as exciting as it is to learn all this information about them, by becoming online friends, they can learn a lot about you too. We need to think about who we share our personal information with, because sometimes we haven't known them long enough for them to earn that trust. So before you accept someone's friend request, you should pause and ask yourself if you want them to know all this information.

You can have someone in your real life without having them in your online life.

Here are some reasons why you might not want to allow someone access to your online life, but still want to be their friend in real life:

● **They post content that isn't good for your mental health (such as things that make you feel bad about your life or the way you look)**

● **They post content that doesn't interest you**

● **They post too much content**

● **They never post so there is no point in following them**

You could also imagine your social media account like a super-exclusive party that only a select few people are allowed to attend. Your followers are your VIP list, and only the very best make the cut. View that 'unfollow' and 'block' button like you are a bouncer putting a little red rope down and denying entry to people who haven't earned the right to see your best pictures.

Just like a party, you get to create your own invite list when it comes to social media. Here are some examples of my list:

INVITED

Close school friends

My godmother

My swimming team

UNINVITED

My sister (she'll tell Dad everything!)

My old teacher

My crush (he'll see too much!)

WHO'S ON YOUR LIST?

Denying people access to your social media, and restricting your access to theirs, is an important boundary to set. When you keep following someone you don't want to follow, you are putting their comfort over your own. You are allowing yourself to feel bad because you're worried they will be hurt or offended if you press that unfollow button. Here's something important to remember: **you can't control someone else's feelings.** Your job is to look after you and surround yourself with things and people that make you happy.

- **Confidence that they can't share information about you with other people**

- **Peace of mind that you don't have to compare your life to theirs**

- **Time, because it's less content to keep up with**

- **Safety, knowing that your privacy is protected**

I've said it already and I'll say it again! Just because you know someone in real life, it doesn't grant them an all-access pass to your online life. Whatever your reason, you don't actually need to share or justify it. It's your page, so it's your choice!

What do you do if they call you out on it? Well, here's a sentence to keep in your back pocket.

'I was changing up who I am following online. It's nothing personal, I still love you, I still care about you, and I still want to be friends. This just means you can update me in real life instead!'

And it works both ways. Just as you unfollowing someone doesn't have to be personal, the same can be said if someone unfollows you. We need to allow everyone the freedom to decide who they want to follow. It doesn't mean anything about your relationship or how close you are, and it's their business. Boundaries always work both ways. If you want other people to respect being denied access to your online world, then you also have to be understanding if you are uninvited to theirs!

If only there was a mute button in real life!

If unfollowing people sounds too scary for you right now, then a temporary fix can be to use the mute button on Instagram, for example. This means you are still following them, but their stories and posts don't come up in your newsfeed any more. To view their content, you need to deliberately go to their page. They won't know they are muted, and you can have peace of mind while you build up the courage to press that unfollow button.

And it really is important that you eventually use the unfollow button over the mute button, because it's a symbol of something greater. The only reason people use the mute button is because they are scared of the other person's feelings, opinions or reaction. And what did we learn in the previous chapter? We cannot control other people's opinions about us – sometimes we just have to do what's right for us. In order to set boundaries in our life, we have to stop being scared of what other people are going to think of us or say about us.

The mute button is a sneaky way to set a boundary, but real-life boundaries can't be sneaky. So use it as a stepping stone, but remember: the end goal is to use the unfollow button . . . and if and when it's necessary, the block button.

That's my business!

Recently, it's become really normal to share everything online. People seem to want to share all the details of their lives, from what they had for breakfast to when they last went to the toilet! But it's OK to say 'NO – I don't want everyone to see and know everything I do.'

You can say:

NO – I don't want to be in that picture.

NO – I don't like that picture, please don't post it online.

NO – I need you to take that photo down. You don't have my permission.

It's important that you ask for permission before you put someone else online, whether it's a photo or a post that tells people their location. Personally, I don't like people knowing my every move. You have to decide the line of what's TMI (too much information). Your parents might want to use the app Find My Friends or location sharing, so they know where you are and can make sure you're safe, but that's different to your friend having it to see what you're up to when you're not with them. This is a boundary you can definitely set!

Make your own rules

This is just the beginning. You can set the boundaries for your online life. I want you to start by asking yourself these questions:

Who do I want to allow access to my social media page?

What behaviour would result in me muting their page?

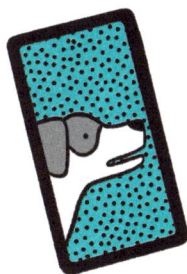

What behaviour would result in me unfollowing them?

What behaviour would result in them being blocked?

Here are my rules:

● **Who can access my social media?**

If someone doesn't have my phone number, they aren't allowed access to my social media. Your social media contains way more information than your phone number does. Your phone number means someone can message you and see your photo on WhatsApp, but social media holds much more private information that I don't want everyone to have. So my rule is: *if I don't trust someone with my phone number, why would I give them more?*

● **What behaviour results in me muting someone?**

This button is for when I want a temporary break from someone. I used this a lot during the Covid-19 pandemic. Everyone coped in different ways and some people coped by posting the scariest stories from the news on their pages. That was NOT helpful to me! But I knew that life would return to normal one day, so I put them on a temporary suspension, otherwise known as the mute button. It's like a short holiday away from that person. So my rule for this button is: *if I need a little holiday from someone, I'll put them on mute.*

- **What behaviour results in me unfollowing someone?**

Let's get into the juicy stuff though . . . what is the line someone needs to cross in order for me to unfollow them? For me, I don't like posts that encourage me to feel bad about my body or the way I look. I worked really hard to like my body and so seeing photos or reading conversations that are negative about certain body types is not good for me. It took me many years to develop a good relationship with food and my body, and so I have to do everything I can to protect that.

Social media can really affect your mental health if you aren't careful. Seeing posts that make you feel bad about yourself can really change the way you think and feel about yourself, and so if a certain person's posts are making you feel rubbish, that's when you need to remember that social media is **your** party and you get to be the bouncer who kicks people out whenever you want! This leads me to my unfollowing rule: *if someone's making me feel bad, it's time to unfollow.*

- **What behaviour results in me blocking someone?**

And finally, the big BLOCK button. The block button is different to the unfollow button because they can't see your stuff at all . . . even if they put your name in the search bar. It's like you don't even exist, so it keeps you extra safe if you don't want a specific person to find you. For me, I use the block button for three purposes:

1) **People who say things on my page that they would never say to my face.**

I have over 200,000 followers, and for some reason a small number of people think it's OK to share their nasty opinions about me on social media. If you are going to be unkind on my page, then you don't deserve the benefit of seeing my content. I'm all up for a healthy debate, but if you follow me and make cruel comments, that's not fair and I don't need that energy in my life.

2) **To help me move on from old relationships.**

When you cut someone out of your life, whether that's a friend or a boyfriend or girlfriend, that also means cutting them out of social media. If you don't, it can make the end of the relationship hurt more, because when you see their happy photos online you may feel sad and regret your decision. And we don't need you torturing yourself over a decision that you made for your own good!

3) **When I am on a platform where I can't control the content I see.**

Such as the For You page on TikTok. Since I can't control what I see coming next, if I end up watching content I don't like, I will first hold down on the screen and click 'not interested'. If that same person comes up on my page again and they are creating content I don't want to see, I will block them.

These are just my rules, though – yours might be different. That's the joy of boundaries: you get to decide your own! Get a piece of paper and draw three boxes like I have here and then fill in those boxes with things people can do that will get them unfollowed, muted and blocked!

Mute if . . .	Unfollow if . . .	Block if . . .

Safety over popularity

We've spoken about times when you might want to limit who can access your online life – whether that's friends, people from school, or even friends of friends. But what about strangers? You are entitled to privacy. What does this mean?

Privacy: The right to keep personal information secret.

This is especially important with strangers, and that includes strangers on the internet. Remember: people aren't always who they say they are, and if someone you don't know is asking you lots of questions about private things, then you need to tell them NO, loud and clear. Deny access to anyone you don't know in real life. In fact, if *anyone* online is asking you for private information, even if it seems to be coming from a friend's account, you still need to be extra careful. You never know who is typing on the other side of the screen.

Here are things that should never be given to strangers on the internet:

- NO to sending your phone number

- NO to telling anyone your home address

- NO to telling people your full name, date of birth or any other details about you

- NO to sharing your exact location

If the person knows you in real life, then you can tell them in person, so there is no reason why anyone should ever want your details online. If you do get asked for personal information, you can say: *'No, I don't share those things online.'* Or: *'No, I don't talk to strangers online, so I am blocking you now.'*

If they ask again, then tell a grown-up – they will be happy you told them and will be able to help you.

Your location also counts as private information. If you post a photo online, only post the picture when you have left the location. For example, if you take a picture of your lunch and you want to tag the restaurant, do it, but only once you've left. It's very easy to forget, when you post in the moment, that one photo can actually provide a lot of information to people online, which dangerous people could then use. Without even meaning to, you could end up showing someone what school you go to, what area you live in and where you hang out on the weekend. This is information that people on the internet should **never** have!

Whatever your boundaries are, it's important to apply them to your online life – especially when you think about how much time you spend on your phone! What you see affects what you think. Changing who you follow and the kind of content you see can be so important for protecting your safety, well-being and mental health. Whether you think of your social media like your home or your exclusive club, the point is the same – **you** can decide who stays and who goes. Just like boundaries are your invisible shield in real life, they are a shield online too in the form of the mute, unfollow and block buttons.

The real world is bigger than the online world

Social media makes it really easy for you to believe your life isn't good enough. It's constant FOMO and comparisons on those apps, and spending too much time on your phone can make you very unhappy. Why do so many of us let these tiny devices dictate our lives? We need to take back control!

The way smartphones are designed has normalized never turning your phone off. With airplane mode and 'do not disturb', we don't even turn our phone off at night or in the cinema. We just put it on silent – but it's not the same thing. By not turning your phone off, you never mentally switch off from it. Back in the day, when I was at school, if I wanted to call a friend, I would have to wait until I got home to use the landline, and sometimes when I called, one of their parents would pick up the phone and I would have to get through an awkward conversation with them before I could chat to my friend. Having to wait until I got home meant that at school, I had a huge physical and mental distance from the phone, which really helped me to concentrate. And there was nothing else you could do with a phone: no games, no texts, no camera!

For secondary school, I went to a boarding school, and there was a rule that we had to turn off our phones every night, hand them in, and we would only be allowed them back after breakfast. I hated it at the time, but what I didn't realize was how much my brain benefited from going to bed without my phone keeping me awake.

Did you know that the blue light from the screens actually makes it harder to sleep? It tells your body to not produce the hormone that makes you sleepy: melatonin. And that's not even counting the amount of hours we delay sleep for ourselves with the endless scrolling. After all, your eyes need to be closed to even try to fall asleep!

NO NO NO NO NO N
O NO NO NO NO NO NO
NO NO NO NO NO N
O NO NO NO NO NO NO
NO NO NO NO NO N
O NO NO NO NO NO NO

So what should we say no to with regard to our phones? How can we give our thumbs a break, give our brains some rest and give our phone a much-needed holiday?

- **Say no to the constant interruptions!**

- **Say no to responding to everyone's demands instantly!**

- **Say no to people having access to you at all hours of the day!**

- **Say no to losing hours of your day scrolling and refreshing!**

Look, I'm the first to appreciate that lots of great things can come from phones and technology. You can find your way if you get lost, you can tell someone if you are running late, and you can catch up with friends even if they are halfway across the world. But it's important to know when enough is enough.

Signs you need a digital detox:

You keep cycling through the apps and you aren't sure what you are even looking for.

You've scrolled the entire feed and there is nothing new to see.

Every picture, post and video you see makes you feel bad about yourself and makes you wish that you were someone else.

Tapping through everyone else's stories convinces you that your life is boring.

The thought of turning off your phone for an hour gives you anxiety.

The first thing you do in the morning and the last thing you do at night is check your phone.

If you start to experience any of these things, then you need to spend some time away from your phone. Your first challenge is to do it for an hour and prove to yourself that nothing awful is going to happen. When someone calls, you don't need to pick up. When someone texts, you don't need to reply immediately. Sometimes when we spend too long on our phones, it's easy to think everything is important or urgent ... but very few things actually are! Sometimes we like to tell ourselves that the people in our lives NEED us. But unless there's something very serious or important happening on that particular day that you know about, then you're probably safe to assume that everyone will survive without you for an hour.

The goal here is to work up to being able to turn your phone off for a day. I'm not telling you to do this because you *should* or because it's *good for you*. I'm telling you to experiment with this because you might find that you are actually happier when you take a break. I'm saying this because I know I am!

Airplane mode — get your head out of the clouds!

Airplane mode is the setting on your phone that is meant to be reserved for being on an aeroplane, but it can be used for so much more than that! It stops the internet, calls and texts working. It basically stops your phone from being a phone, but you can still access your music, pictures, audiobooks and anything that is offline and saved on to it. It's actually one of my favourite tools to use! Do you find that whenever you're just about to pick up a good book, suddenly in the corner of your eye you catch a glimpse of your phone sitting there. Or how about the moment you sit down to actually get your homework done? That shiny black screen on our phones is just always so ... tempting! Fact: I never finish a chapter of a book unless my phone is on airplane mode.

One thing I've learned to do is make sure I create some time every day to have my phone on airplane mode. Sometimes I will go for a walk or have a bath with my music playing. This gives my mind a much-needed breather from the constant scrolling and comparing.

Outside of airplane mode, you can control access on a smaller scale. And people can have different amounts of access! Did you know there are settings on social media and your phone to help you out? You can do all these things without anyone knowing. Here are a few ...

- **Select a handful of people who are exempt when your phone is on 'do not disturb'– this means the most important people are able to contact you, whether it's your parents or your best friend.**

- **Archive a conversation on WhatsApp if you don't want notifications from a particular person or group chat, or change the settings on your phone so only certain apps give you notifications at all.**

- **Set a screen time limit for certain apps. When you've been on the app for that amount of time, a message pops up to tell you you've had enough.**

Life is happening right now. Look up before you miss it!

One of the best things about creating boundaries with my phone and putting a little distance between myself and social media is realizing how many times I was letting my phone distract me from **real-life moments**.

Have you ever found yourself missing parts of a conversation because you were too busy peeking at someone on social media? You can look through your phone when you're alone, but when you start to do it around other people, you end up missing out on fun and interesting experiences and conversations.

Setting boundaries with my phone has also helped me recognize the value in not documenting everything. My job is to post on social media, but four years into being an influencer, I remember catching myself during my sister's wedding. I had been so busy documenting it on Snapchat that I actually struggled to remember many parts of it that weren't in the videos and pictures I took. I ended up living through one of the most exciting days of mine and my family's life through a screen! From that day on, I promised myself to live life more in the moment. Yes, I can take a quick picture and even a video occasionally, but then the phone goes away! Doing this has made my conversations better, my memories fuller and my days more fun. Ask yourself the following:

- **Have you ever missed a whole conversation because you were glued to your screen?**

- **Have you ever spent so long getting the perfect selfie that you forgot to properly catch up with friends?**

- **Have you ever struggled to focus on the fun you are having because you're looking through social media and wondering what other people are doing instead?**

If the answer is yes, then you need to rethink how and when you use your phone.

A Christmas challenge

It's important to check your screen time once in a while. I know parents moan at you about this and they are no better ... Everyone, no matter what age, could do with evaluating how much screen time is a healthy amount. You don't need to wait for your parents to make the rules – you need your own set of rules.

I'd like to challenge you to turn your phone off over the Christmas break. I do it every year, so we can do it together! It could be for just a couple of hours, or one day – but I'm going to try for a week and see how it feels. It could be the best

DO NOT OPEN UNTIL 26TH DECEMBER

present we ever give ourselves. It's giving your brain the gift of a holiday, free from comparison, free from overthinking and free from feeling like you have to share everything going on in your life at all times!

When your screen time goes down, you might even discover a new hobby. It forces you to find other ways to have fun and also makes you realize how much time you TRULY spend scrolling your life away. And what's even better is that when you get your phone back, the stuff that usually affects you so much doesn't hit as hard. It's like the time away from your phone creates the emotional distance to realize that the real world is much bigger than your online world.

We can't let these shiny black screens dictate our lives and how we feel. Setting boundaries with our phones can help us feel happier, sleep better and boost our confidence. So next time you are mid-scroll and you get those twinges that make you feel bad about yourself, I want you to stop, put your phone down and go do something else. Anything else!

Here are some ideas:

- **Do ten jumping jacks.**

- **Put on your favourite song and don't pick up your phone until the song is over!**

- **Go make a snack or a drink and don't pick your phone up until it's finished.**

I refuse to watch the blue ticks of validation

Have you ever sent a message and wanted a reply so desperately that you stare at your screen, just waiting for the message to send and the response to come through? On some messaging apps, you can watch your message as it goes from one grey tick to show it's been sent, to two grey ticks to show it's been delivered, and then finally the ticks turn blue to show that the person has read the message.

If those blue ticks don't appear, you might be tempted to check when they were last online (as this information is provided on some apps). In fact, it can even show you if the person is online right now. It can feel like torture!

Maybe the app that tortures you is Instagram instead, where you can swipe up on your story as the names fill in and see who is watching it AND how quickly they are watching it?

We can waste so much time refreshing apps, worrying about whether people are ignoring us, wondering if they screenshotted your story or simply flicked through it while scrolling on the toilet. And it's all quite rough on our mental health. How can we stop obsessing?!

The first trick is to remember that the world doesn't revolve around us. Someone's silence doesn't have to mean something personal against us. I know it's rare, but they just might not be on their phone. Although it's easy to imagine stories in your head about them being secretly angry at you, it's also easy to come up with other possibilities. Maybe they are with their parents? Maybe they are at the cinema? Maybe they are napping? Try to check yourself when your brain jumps to the worst possible reason and think about all the other more likely reasons they might not be replying.

Everyone will have a different relationship with their phones; some people will pick up after one ring and some people are so slow to respond that they might as well not have a phone at all. But what can you do when someone's lack of replies is doing your head in?

If you really feel like someone is ignoring you, you can politely ask for a reply:

'I don't know if you saw my last message, but a reply would be great!'

If someone doesn't message you as much as you would like them to, tell them:

'We rarely text any more and I miss you. Can we catch up soon?'

If you are worried that they are angry at you, let them know:

'You've been acting a bit differently lately, and I was wondering if you are OK?'

Your phone can't be the boss of you

and you can't let other people's behaviour with their phones rule your life either.

You need to figure out what your own boundaries are and what works for you. Good boundaries means understanding that just because you've sent a message doesn't mean you are owed an immediate reply. I'm sure there are plenty of times when you've not replied to a message because you're busy, but when others do the same, you assume they're angry with you!

I remember one of my friends getting really upset with me one day for 'ignoring' her message and when I explained I was busy, she said she could see I was online. But I was only online because I was trying to find the person I was meeting up with, and I wasn't replying to anyone apart from that one person! The silence was not personal. Do you see what I mean when I say . . .

The world doesn't revolve around you.

By setting good boundaries, you will be less fixated on how quickly people reply to you. And you'll remember that:

You are the one in charge!

● **If you find yourself watching the grey ticks turn blue, there is usually a setting that you can switch off. It means the ticks stay grey whether someone has read the message or not, which can free your mind from worrying about it.**

- If you don't want people to know whether you are online on Instagram, go to your privacy settings, look for Activity Status and make sure it's off.

- If you find yourself checking when someone was last online, there is a setting in WhatsApp where you can turn off your 'last seen'! People won't be able to see when you were last online, and you won't be able to see when they were either.

- Say no to caring if someone is online.

- Say no to watching messages being read.

- Say no to pausing your life and waiting by the phone.

You are important to someone!

The harsh truth is that we all have our own list of priorities and there are people who we will reply to more quickly than others. It's weird how we only tend to notice when we are lower down on someone's list, and it's really easy to forget or appreciate that there are lots of people in the world who will always put us first.

Let's change that mindset. Let's think about the people who DO put us first.

Who are the people who make you happiest? How do they make you feel loved?

There are many people who care about you in this world and sometimes it's easy to not notice them. Next time you see them, why don't you tell them how much you appreciate them and thank them for always caring about you. A little bit of gratitude goes a long way.

Likes do not equal popularity!

As we've discussed, social media can make you think bad things about yourself. Whether it's how many likes you get on a post or how many followers you have compared with your friends, social media can make you think you are unpopular, unloved or not good enough. I know being on social media can sometimes feel like a popularity contest, but numbers are not a way to measure worth.

- If you look at other people's pictures and think they look better than you, remember that there is probably someone who is thinking the same thing about you.

- If you look at other people's posts and think they look happier than you, it's likely that someone will be thinking the same thing about you.

- If you look at the number of followers someone has and think they are more popular than you, perhaps someone will be thinking the same thing about you.

You know this from being on social media yourself . . . Social media only shows half of what's going on in your life. I posted a happy smiling picture online when I found out my dad had cancer. I posted a happy smiling picture online when my best friend had just broken up with me.

I share my scars, not my wounds, online.

If something in my life is hurting me, I don't always want to share all my feelings online and open that wound to the world. You want to keep that wound protected. Once it's healed and formed a scar, it then has a layer of protection round it. This is when I feel I can tell people about it, because it's not as raw as it was when it was a wound. For example, if I have just had an argument with my friend and I am upset about it, social media is not the best place to go. If I start sharing the details of the fight with everyone, it can get really messy! Once I have resolved the disagreement, though, that's when it's safe to go back on to social media. By waiting until the wounds have healed, you protect yourself and your friendship too.

When I was a teen, I thought that if I had a certain level of popularity, all my dreams would come true. I thought that the people who were popular, either in school or online, must have the best lives. That was until one day in school, when a popular girl decided to sit with me at lunch. It was probably because there was no one else from our year group in the dining hall, so we were stuck with each other. In our short conversation, I realized how even though she was much more popular than me, she was still just like me. She still worried about her homework, friendship dramas and everything else that I worried about. Talking to her made me realize that being in the cool group was not as perfect as it seemed. Our short chat actually made me thankful for the friends I had. And the same goes for the online world. Having followers is fun, but people with a lot of followers are just like you and me. They have their own problems, even if they don't show it online, and **likes aren't everything**. Real friends, the real world and real experiences are what will truly bring you joy.

Whether it's being popular online, getting the most likes on Instagram or the most followers on TikTok, all these things are fleeting. They are not reliable! They all give you something called **external validation**, which means your feelings of happiness are coming from the outside and can be taken away. What we need more of is **internal validation**, which comes from the inside. It's much harder for people to take away your internal validation! Want some of that? Let me show you how . . .

When you have a major win in life:

● External validation is posting a picture of it on social media and waiting for the likes to come pouring in.

● Internal validation is telling yourself, 'Wow, I'm so proud of myself, that's amazing.'

When your friends think what you are wearing is weird:

● External validation is getting changed and then asking if your new outfit is better.

● Internal validation is saying 'well, I like it, so that's all that matters.'

When your picture on social media gets no likes:

● External validation is deleting the picture and hoping no one saw you got zero likes.

- **Internal validation is knowing you posted the photo because it made you happy.**

Internal validation means knowing your opinion is more important than anyone else's. Internal validation means knowing you are good enough without the replies, likes and followers. Internal validation means knowing that building up your self-esteem is **your** job!

And you don't need to deprive yourself of external validation to enjoy the perks of internal validation. External validation is not a bad thing, you just don't want to rely on it, as feeling good from the inside is so important. So enjoy your wins and successes and happy moments privately. Realize you can be proud of yourself without anyone else's approval. And then share your amazing news with the world!

When we know the difference between external validation and internal validation, it's easier to become aware of when we are reaching for our phones for a validation boost. Once we're aware of this, we can set healthy boundaries with our phones that allow us to feel good, confident, well-rested and happy!

Ten rules for boundaries with your phone

1. You can unfollow, block and mute anyone you want to

2. You don't have to be on social media just because other people are

3. Remember: the real world is bigger than the online world

4. Step away from social media when it makes you feel bad

5. Don't give out private information on the internet to people you don't know

6. Ask permission before posting pictures of others

7. Be selective about who gets a ticket to your social media party

8. You don't have to reply to a text the moment you see it

9. If you wouldn't say it to someone's face, don't say it online

10. Remember that not everything you see online is real

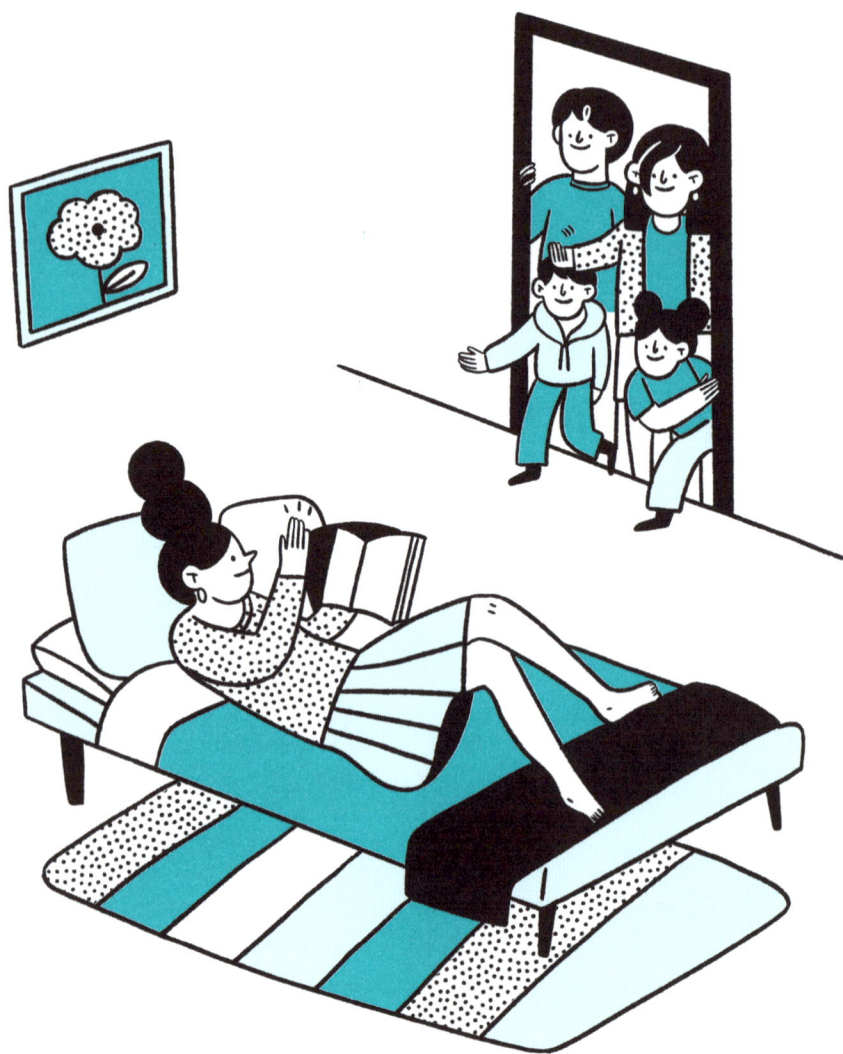

Chapter 3

Saying no to family

- How do I stop my siblings from going into my room without my permission?

- What do I do if my parents want me to take sides in their arguments?

- Why are my siblings always taking my things?

- How do I get my parents to respect my privacy?

- How do I respond to 'my house, my rules'?

- Why are other families normal and mine is not?

Now, I've really buried this one deep in the book so your parents or carers don't see it in here – I'm sure they don't want me telling you that you can say no to your family too! But it's so important to have boundaries with your family. If you wouldn't tolerate something from someone else, then don't tolerate it from them! They don't get a free-for-all pass just because they are related to you. It can sometimes be really hard to set boundaries with family – they've known you the longest, and often, they know you the best. But as you grow up and change and evolve as a person, you deserve the right to set some rules that make you comfortable. Don't get me wrong: as annoying as it is to hear, our parents are there to look after us and even when we disagree with them, they usually have our

best interests at heart. Part of the power of 'no' is knowing the right time to use it and when we should listen. After all, if we want them to listen to our boundaries, then we also have to listen when they set boundaries with us.

Before I start this chapter, it's important to mention that families can come in all shapes and sizes. You might have a mum, dad and siblings. Or two mums and no siblings. Or two dads and twenty-five siblings! Or your family might come with divorce and step-parents, or maybe your grandparents raised you instead of your parents. Perhaps you have adopted parents, carers or guardians. Every family is different and valid, and no one is better or worse than the other.

Siblings: the house-mates you never asked for

Siblings can be the best friends you never chose, but for some, it's more a case of the housemates you never asked for. It's the way they know exactly what to do to annoy you in that very specific way that even friends can't. Some lucky people have amazing relationships with their siblings, but some people have more difficult relationships with their brothers and sisters, and that's OK, because families are complicated! Some people are close to one sibling but not another, and some don't have any siblings at all.

Love them or hate them, siblings can really help you build up your 'no' muscle, because – let's be honest – they tend to test it a lot. When it comes to families, they know us best and that can make it really difficult to change as everyone is expecting you to act the same as you always have done. This is why it can be particularly frustrating as a younger sibling, when your older siblings treat you like a baby – when you are CLEARLY not a baby any more. But now that you have your 'no' superpower and your trusty invisible shield of boundaries, things can change! We've got big dreams and plans for you now. Nothing can defeat you – even brothers and sisters with their super-sneaky sibling tactics!

Siblings have an extraordinary ability to get under your skin in a way no one else can. You know those toys that you wind up and they start jiggling? Well, humans are a lot like that too, and siblings know that. It's like we have a button that says 'wind up' – siblings just press it and press it and press it, and then before you know it you snap and they've won! You took the bait, they got under your skin, you are angry, annoyed and screaming, and they are laughing. And of course, who gets in trouble . . . YOU DO! Not fair.

It would be perfect if adults could see everything, so they knew when to step in, but if your siblings are particularly sneaky, they'll manage to get away without being caught. You know what, though? You don't have to wait for the grown-ups. Now that you are older, you've got the power (and the confidence!) to set boundaries yourself. You can fight your own battles, you can tell your siblings to stop – and you can say NO.

Fart in your own room, not mine!

You know when you get in trouble at school, and you get punished – maybe with detention or additional homework? That's a consequence. There can be good consequences too. If you behave well, you might get compliments, praise or maybe even a reward. Well, boundaries are no different. When you set a boundary with your siblings, you can set a consequence for if they refuse to stop doing the thing that's crossing the boundary. For example, let's say your sister keeps farting in your room (we've all been there . . .). You could say: *'You wouldn't like it if I farted in your room so don't fart in mine. If you keep farting in my room, I'm not going to let you in any more!'*

If they keep doing it, then you can do something called reinforcing the boundary. Imagine you are losing at tug of war, and you need more people on your team as reinforcement to stand behind you and provide additional support. That's exactly the same when you are reinforcing your boundaries, but instead of adding more people to your team, you are giving yourself more support by standing by what you said and repeating it. This way, they know that **you mean business**!

Sometimes when you set boundaries for the first time, the people who have known you longest might be shocked and surprised. They don't know this new you! And they might not even be sure if this new you is here to stay. When you reinforce the boundary, it's like being your own back-up. When you repeat what you've said, what you are really saying is, 'My boundary is here to stay! You better get used to it!'

But how do you reinforce it? Try saying:

'I've told you once and I will say it again. If you fart in my room one more time, I am going to start locking my door.'

This is when you might get one of these replies:

'You're too sensitive!'
'You don't have a sense of humour!'
'Learn to take a joke!'

Well, you aren't too sensitive.
You do have a sense of humour.
And you know how to take a joke . . . when it's funny!

Your siblings (and people in general) say things like this when you call them out because they don't know how to communicate how they really feel. And so they squeeze out all their frustration and guilt into aggressive and unsympathetic comments like this.

But just remember that if something they are doing – whether it's farting in your room or making unkind comments – makes you uncomfortable or hurts your feelings, then this is valid! Even if they didn't intend to hurt your feelings. And even if the thing you're getting upset about seems petty (which is often the way in sibling arguments). If they care about you, then when you tell them that you are upset, they should care too. Whether or not you get an apology from your sibling, I want you to know with every cell of your body that you were right. You can't help being upset by certain actions or words and if it makes you feel bad, you are allowed to feel that way. How you feel is important!

When you speak up for your emotions, say no to people being mean to you and set boundaries around how you deserve to be treated, your confidence and self-esteem will grow. When you know you deserve to be treated with kindness, it's easier to treat yourself with kindness too!

R-E-S-P-E-C-T: Find out what it means to me!

If you don't get the reference in the title, then you need to get online and look up the song 'Respect' by Aretha Franklin. This is your boundaries anthem. Let it ring in your ears as you stand up for yourself and say no. Boundaries are all about respect. You deserve to be respected and that means you also have to respect others. Respect is a two-way street.

RESPECT

Relationships with the adults in your life can be complicated. Some people have very affectionate parents or carers who would do absolutely anything for them. For others, the people who look after them might be quite strict and show their love in a different way. Some grown-ups want to know everything that their child is doing in order to help keep them safe. Others let them be more independent, as they believe they have to learn lessons for themselves.

Your relationship with your parents or carers might be different to your friend's relationship with theirs, but that doesn't make your family weird or their family normal. Every family will have different rules and different ways of viewing the world. Some people might say that parents deserve respect because they are parents, but actually that's not quite true. They deserve respect because they are **human**!

When I was growing up, I was always told that you should 'respect your elders'. And my brother, who is only 362 days older than me (not even a whole year!) used to claim that meant he counted as an elder and that I had to respect him. Now that I'm a bit older, I can finally admit that he was right. Not about him being older, I should add! I should have respected him because **everyone deserves respect**, no matter how old they are, no matter how much you like them (or don't like them!), no matter whether you even know them or not! Respecting someone doesn't mean you have to like them. Respecting someone means that you treat them in a way that you want to be treated.

When it comes to your family, it means:

- **Living peacefully alongside each other even when you sometimes wish you could just be alone.**

- **Being polite, even after you've had a bad day.**

- **Understanding that the mutual space in the house belongs to all of you, and so you should tidy up after yourself.**

Living under the same roof as your parents can be a tough one. Have you ever been told that you treat the place like a hotel? Haven't we all! Well . . . one thing that really helped change my relationship with my parents (and stopped them driving me mad with that phrase!) was thinking about how I would treat a friend's house and doing the same in my own house. Look, I know it's easy to become lazy in our own home, and get used to everything being done for us like when we were younger. But you are growing up now, and that means things have to change.

My thinking was, 'I want to be treated like an adult so I've gotta act like one!' If I had dinner at a friend's house, I would always offer to help get the table ready, and after dinner I would take my plates to the kitchen. If I spilled a drink at a friend's house, I would go get a towel to clean it up and not just rub it in with my foot (well, most of the time . . .).

If we are being honest with ourselves, lots of us can probably admit that we treat our friends' houses better than we treat our own.

Being respectful is a way to earn respect.

Maybe you're thinking that respect sounds kind of boring! But part of growing up is understanding that if you don't want people treating you or your stuff badly, you can't treat them or their stuff badly either. And realizing the importance of respect is the first step to forming those all-important boundaries.

You shouldn't have to go to space to get some space!

Now don't get me wrong: I understand that setting rules with your family isn't always easy. Like I've said before, being your age is hard. You are constantly told to give respect but sometimes it feels like no one gives **YOU** any! There's nothing worse than hearing the phrase 'you're too young to understand'. Rude! Or 'my house, my rules'. Or how about the classic: 'as long as you are under my roof . . . ' And don't get me started on 'because I say so'. My eyes are rolling too. You deserve to be treated with respect. We can't control how other people behave though – the only thing we can own is how we behave. But I understand that sometimes it feels impossible to control your behaviour when someone provokes you picks a fight.

I WOZ HERE

Often, when I'm in the heat of the moment in an argument, I have all these big feelings, and I'll be honest with you, they can make me really confused. I don't know what I want to say, I don't know how I feel and then I just end up blurting out the first thing I can think of . . . and usually it's not very nice. Ultimately, I'm just struggling to say what I'm really thinking, which is that I feel very vulnerable. (Like that awful dream where you turn up to school naked!) Or that I'm feeling really ganged-up on. And of course, if you feel attacked, you're going to defend yourself! So what's a good thing to do instead of going into defence mode?

Ask for space

You could say something like: 'This is a lot right now; I'm going to go to my room for five minutes and can we continue when I come back down?' Or: 'I need to pause. I'm going to go and take a breather and I'll let you know when I'm ready to talk again.' Then you can go to your room, and if you're anything like me, you might end up having a little cry. I cry nearly every week, and when my feelings are huge, the best release for me is to just let those tears out.

For some people, it can be really nice to go for a walk instead of going to their room. Others like to listen to angry music and scream into a pillow. You need to find your feel-good release. It's like the argument has blown up a balloon inside you that's filled with hot air, and when you get the space you need, you can deflate the balloon before it POPS.

Then when you are ready, you can pick up the conversation again. All you have to say is:

- 'I'm ready to talk now!'

- 'I've had some time to think and what I was feeling was . . .'

- 'Can we go back to the conversation we were having earlier?'

No matter what the outcome of the conversation is, you can be proud of yourself for taking some time out to feel your feelings. And taking that time definitely increases the chance of a more productive conversation about how to respect each other's boundaries in your family.

If we all thought the same, the world would be boring!

Sometimes when someone is older than you, they think that they know better than you. They've been around longer than you, so the chances are they probably do know quite a bit more, simply from having more life experience. But I also believe you can learn something new from **everyone**. Different brains work in different ways and as you grow up, it can be hard for parents or carers to realize that you are your own separate person with different thoughts and beliefs to them. So sometimes it can be helpful to remind them that you are growing up and are able to make your own decisions about certain things.

But this doesn't mean you won't still need their help at times. You might feel like you know everything, and you do know **WAYYY** more than you did when you were younger, but your brain is still developing, and your parents or carers are there to help you out as you learn more about the world. It's important to listen to them, as sometimes their way of doing things is safer ... even if you can't see it! The key to using the word 'no' is knowing when to listen to your parents' no and when to use your own no.

Most of the time, adults are really trying to look out for you, so if you want them to hear you when you speak, you have to hear them out too. Why are they telling you no? Is it for your own safety? Trust me when I tell you that most parents don't *want* to be a party pooper. It's their job to worry about boring things such as your safety, so you can focus on having fun – and that's why sometimes what you want to do conflicts with what they are telling you to do. You might not see the danger in the fun option . . . but thankfully, they do! They can see the bigger picture and what's important, and as annoying as it is sometimes, we all need to try and remember that (myself included!).

The right time to listen to their no:

- **When you might be in danger.**

- **When you need to be somewhere on time.**

- **When something concerns your health or well-being.**

- When you could hurt someone else.

- When they are advising you on something they know more about.

- When they are asking you to be respectful.

In an ideal world, we listen to them and they listen to us, and then we all win, because we all feel respected and are each aware of the other's boundaries! Everyone else's no is just as important as yours. They have boundaries too and we want to make sure we are treating them as we would want to be treated ourselves!

But what if you feel it's not the right time to listen to your parents' no?

This can happen sometimes, and that's OK. You just need to have a conversation about it. Ask them to explain to you why they are saying no. Tell them you would love to know the reason and what you might find is that, even if you don't like their reason, it will make sense. Sometimes we focus on what we want so closely that we can't see the wider picture of why we can't just do what we want when we want to. And if it makes you feel any better, even adults, with all their freedom, can rarely do that either! Can you imagine if your teachers turned up to school in pyjamas simply because they wanted to? (No one wants to see that!)

There might be occasions when you do decide it's time to fight your corner because something is particularly important to you. You're at a prime age right now for parents or carers not understanding you – they might still see you as the child you were a few years ago, and not realize that the things you like and care about have changed. But the good news is that someone doesn't have to understand your boundaries in order to respect them.

Let's say your mum doesn't understand why you get so upset when she moves things around in your room. Maybe she doesn't understand why you want things to be in a certain place, and maybe she doesn't need to know why. What she does need to know, though, is that this matters to you and that's a big enough reason.

There are so many moments in my childhood where I wish I could go back and explain to my mum:

'This is important to me. You don't have to understand why, but please stop what you are doing.'

Or:

'My way of doing things might not be your way of doing things and – as long as no one's getting hurt – that's OK.'

I can't even tell you the number of arguments and tears it would've saved! I don't live in fantasyland, though. I know family conversations don't always end in resolution and that can be really frustrating! It can be so unfair when it feels like there is one rule for one family member and a different rule for another. It can also be unfair when someone doesn't want to talk about it with you. Your family might not always see your side of things, and they might not even be *trying* to see your side of things, but that doesn't mean that you are a bad person in any way. But as long as you are trying your best to be fair and respectful, you can know your intentions are good! And even though it can be really hard to respect someone when you feel like they don't respect you, it's important you continue to be respectful . . . not for them, but for YOU! You want to be proud of your behaviour, no matter how the other person has acted. You know those times when you get into an argument and someone makes a horrible comment and then before you know it, an insult has flown out of your mouth too?

It never feels very good, does it? I know you want to yell, 'But they started it!' And you are right, they did! But if you sink to their level, then you are no better.

Hold your head high and keep that crown on straight, and know that no one can drag you into the mud unless you let them!

There are a few 'no's that I live by with my family, to show that we respect each other:

No to yelling!

No to insults!

No to name-calling!

No to body shaming!

No to entering rooms without asking!

No to borrowing things without permission!

Your turn! What 'no's are important to you with your family? When you have decided which 'no's are important to you, you can talk to a parent or carer and ask them whether, together, you can come up with a list of family 'no's. It can be a great idea to have the whole family sit down and talk through what is important to each person. Then your list of family boundaries can hang somewhere in the house so everyone can see them every day! Coming up with boundaries together can be an amazing way to make sure everyone feels heard and understood.

Not my business, not my problem

I was such a busybody growing up. I used to be involved in everyone's business and I loved that people would share things with me, both good and bad. Well, I'm a life coach now – people share their issues with me, and I help them resolve those issues – so I guess things haven't changed that much! But what I do know now is when to get involved and when not to. Because if you end up getting involved in every fight and every drama, especially the ones that have nothing to do with you, you will be exhausted. After all, you have lots of your own things to focus your energy on!

The arguments I hated the most were the ones between my parents. I always found it scary when my parents fought. I would imagine the worst and I never knew if this fight would end with them getting a divorce.

Now, this part might not be for everyone. If your parents don't bring you into their arguments, then you might not need to read this. But this is for the people who have ever felt trapped in-between both their parents. This is for anyone who has been asked to take sides. It's an awful feeling! You can't win, because if you choose one person, then you will hurt the other person's feelings, and if you don't choose either, the arguing could just keep going on! When this used to happen to me, this is what I wish I knew:

It is not your job to fix your parents' marriage!

You don't need to be your parents' therapist! No child should ever have to pick sides and you are allowed to opt out entirely. They are adults and part of their job is to take care of you, not for you to take care of them. I know that sounds unbalanced, and you might feel guilty when you say no to picking sides, but they are fully equipped to handle their own problems. And although it can feel really bad to see someone you love in pain, that doesn't make it your job to get involved. Their marriage problems should not become entire family problems. You aren't going to become a marriage counsellor overnight and nor should you have to!

So how do you opt out? Well, when my parents ask me to take sides, I will often say . . .

'This doesn't involve me. You have an issue with Mum/Dad, so you have to talk to them about it.'

Or you can be even firmer and say . . .

'I need both of you to stop talking to me about your marriage problems. It's not fair and I love both of you, so I don't want to pick sides. I'm going to leave the room so you can sort it yourselves.'

Just because you don't want to get involved, it doesn't mean you don't care! Let's say you have a problem with your mum. The only way to resolve the problem is to talk to your mum about it directly. Talking to your dad or your sibling might allow you to vent, but often it makes it more complicated as everyone else will have opinions and possibly take sides. The same goes for your parents! Talking to you or your siblings about it just makes the problem bigger. If you ever have an issue with **one person**, talk to that **one person!**

The worst part about family fights was that they made me really embarrassed that my family wasn't perfect like other's. But all families fight, and I remember the day I learned this.

It was Christmas Day, and everyone had got into an argument over presents. It started because my brother had asked me what I wanted for Christmas a few weeks before, and I told him I wasn't sure what I *did* want, but I knew exactly what I *didn't* want. On Christmas morning, I unwrapped my present and I was so annoyed to find he had bought me the exact thing I had said I didn't want. My parents obviously didn't know we had already had this conversation, and they thought I was being ungrateful, which made me even angrier. Furious, I stormed off to my room.

I was sitting on my bed when I got a text from one of my best friends saying 'Happy Christmas!' and asking how my day was

going. For the first time in my life, I was honest about how I was fighting with my family and that actually, I had locked myself in my room because I was so angry at **everyone**. And to my amazement, she replied saying she was doing the **exact same thing!** She had also got in a fight with her brother and locked herself in her room. The only difference was that she had her dog for company. We both joked that we wished we

were together so we could have fun on Christmas and forget our families!

And then I asked her, 'Why have you never told me that you fight with your family?' She replied: 'Why haven't you ever told me you fight with yours?' We both felt silly because neither of us had mentioned it for the same reason. We were both embarrassed and thought there was something wrong with our families. We were especially embarrassed because it was Christmas Day, which is the day when there's so much pressure to be a perfect family!

We spoke about how we felt like failures who couldn't live up to the perfect Christmas Day. Eventually, we realized that talking to each other was the best present we could give each other moving forward. We made a promise to each other that the next time our families got into a fight and we were upset about it, we would tell the other person! We helped each other feel less alone and discovered how there's no shame in having an imperfect family.

If you want to have boundaries in your life, you need to be OK with conflict and realize that no family is perfect. Everyone argues, and you can become a stronger unit as a result. Sometimes when you set boundaries, it is easy and effortless, and sometimes it is a little tougher and there are disagreements. Just because you disagree, it doesn't mean you don't love each other. Your feelings towards arguing are often based on your upbringing. So, if you grew up in a household where there was fighting, you might feel scared of conflict. Then, as you grow older, you might try to avoid conflict entirely, and that's how a people-pleaser is born. But you need to understand that although it's easier to say yes in the short term, it's important to say no and honour your true feelings. This will help you feel happier in the long term, as people will be able to understand and respect your boundaries. Ignoring how you feel or brushing it under the carpet will just create more issues later, so we need to be brave and voice our feelings . . . no matter how scary it is!

Ten rules for boundaries with your family

1. Families don't require different boundaries just because they're family

2. Knock before entering someone's room

3. You do not need to get involved in fights that aren't yours

4. Everyone deserves respect, because they are human, not because of age

5. Even if you disagree with your parents, hear them out and think carefully about whether they have your best interests at heart

6. You are allowed to ask for space if an argument gets too heated

7. Ask before borrowing anyone else's things

8. Being respectful is a way to earn respect

9. You are not your parents' therapist

10. Every family fights and that's OK!

Chapter 4
Saying no at school

- When can I say no to a teacher – and how do I do it?!

- Why am I always overwhelmed with homework?

- How do I find time for school and my friends?

- What should I say when a teacher is telling me off for something I didn't do?

- How do I get the people in my group project to pull their weight?

119

Ahhh, school. Now this is a tough one. We're sent off to school for most of our weeks and told to sit down, be quiet and that teachers are always right. But sometimes it doesn't feel fair. What if the teacher is wrong about something? And what if you want to stand up for yourself? If school is meant to nurture independent thinking, so that we become adults who can use our voices to stand up for our beliefs, then why does it feel like we can't act that way when we're actually AT school? There's an important balance to strike here between knowing what's fair and knowing when to respect the rules and not get yourself in trouble. So how do you find that magical tipping point where you are allowed to have thoughts and opinions, and more importantly, express those thoughts and opinions?

And that isn't the only difficult part of school to navigate. It can be really stressful as a young person trying to find time for your friends and your homework when most of your day is eaten up by school hours. So the challenge here is finding your voice, figuring out a way to feel like yourself at school, standing up for what's right, and all while having enough time to rest, hang out with friends, do extracurricular activities and juggle *everything* else. Well, do not fear, I am here to help!

Only monsters scream!

Teachers can be tricky! They are bigger, older and they tend to want things done their way and only their way. It's hard to believe they were once like us – students sitting in a classroom – and were the ones having to do the listening and learning. Similarly to parents, they are the ones who create all the rules, but it's a little more difficult for teachers because they don't just have a few kids, they have many, *many* more to deal with. As a result, they might not always listen to you or take the time to see things from your point of view. Your parents are the bosses at home; teachers are the bosses at school. But even teachers have their own bosses, so they can't always do things the way they want, either!

I remember when I was in sixth form, I finally felt as though teachers were treating us as their equals. And that was when I figured out – woahhh, weird – teachers are just like us! Some are even funny! Some are people I would actually want to be friends with! But until you get to that point, they often just feel like the people handing out all the rules and stopping all the fun. It's a difficult relationship to navigate.

Teachers are really smart – they have all the information and are the ones who will help you pass your exams. They studied hard and did well at school to become teachers, and so when it comes to learning, you have to trust that they know what they're talking about. But – and you might want to sit down for this one – teachers aren't always right. Just like you and me, they are still human. And no human in the world can be right every single time (even me!). And sometimes being wrong comes in the form of shouting or losing their temper. In the same way that respect is a two-way street with our parents, respect should also be mutual at school. Yes, it's important that you follow the rules, go to class on time and behave in lessons, BUT it doesn't mean that your teachers can speak to you however they want to. You deserve respect as well!

Outside of school, it's never OK for someone to shout and scream. And I want you to know, if someone shouts at you in school, that is also not OK. You should never speak to anyone that way and you should never have to raise your voice in order to be heard. Shouting is rude and unkind and when it comes from someone bigger than yourself, it can be really scary. Although it is really important to listen to other people, teachers included, you are allowed to say no to teachers raising their voice at you. Here are some things you could say that are polite, confident and fair when someone yells at you . . .

'Please stop yelling at me. Can you speak to me at a lower volume?'

If they carry on yelling, I want you to know that you don't need to feel intimidated – remember it's about **them** and not **you**. Let them own their bad behaviour while you keep acting according to your own values and morals – you can be proud of the person you are!

Sometimes it isn't yelling that makes you feel bad. Sometimes it's because they put you on the spot and ask you to answer a question in front of everyone. It feels really unfair because if you knew the answer, you would have put your hand up . . . but you didn't. And now everyone is staring at you, the teacher is waiting and it can feel really embarrassing. You could always take a guess if you feel confident doing so, but if you have no idea what the answer is, then it's OK to say that too. If they pick on you when you don't know the answer, say:

'I don't know the answer, please will you explain?'

Sometimes you might get told off for attempting to answer a question and then getting it wrong. If that does happen, first of all, please know it's OK to make mistakes. But if you are being shamed for making a mistake, you can say something such as:

'I know I made a mistake, and I am sorry. I will try to do better next time, but right now this is making me feel bad.'

If you set a boundary in a calm, polite and confident way such as this, then you're doing the right thing!

If you are respectful to everyone, then it's your right to demand respect back.

Now, I can't promise that a teacher will always listen to you or your boundaries. Perhaps they've had a bad day and feel like no one has been listening to *them*. Or perhaps they don't yet understand your boundaries. And this can be difficult and make you feel stuck.

I remember when this happened to me. When I was young, I *hated* being told off. But one day at school, there was a girl who kept being rude to me every time the teacher's back was turned. I put up my hand to tell the teacher but couldn't get my words out properly, my brain glitched and I forgot the word 'mouthed'. I ended up saying, 'Emily is saying mean words but she isn't actually saying them.' Of course, the teacher had no idea what I was talking about and decided I was wasting her time, so I ended up getting in trouble instead. I got yelled at for making things up about Emily and it felt rubbish. If I could go back and tell my younger self something, though, it would be that I am still proud of her for saying something. Despite the outcome, she was right to stand up for herself. The teacher didn't understand me that day, but I can feel confident in the belief that I was respectful and did nothing wrong.

If a teacher keeps treating you unfairly or yelling at you, you can get help from another adult. You are not alone, and someone will be happy to step in. Speak to a parent or guardian about it and tell them what you are going through. You don't have to cope with it all on your own and **it's really brave to ask for help.** When your boundaries are not being listened to, it's OK to ask another adult to help you reinforce your boundary. It's like if you mess with a bear cub, you'll have the big bear to deal with!

Done is better than perfect

We can't have good boundaries without good communication skills. Good communication means being direct and avoiding lying simply because it makes your life easier. In other words, having good boundaries means saying no when you mean no and saying yes when you mean yes. It means doing what you say and saying what you do.

So far, we have focused on setting boundaries and standing up for yourself when you're being mistreated. And we have talked about how to treat others well too. So much of boundaries is about **respect,** and in order to treat people with respect, we have to be honest and reliable. We can't expect people to tell us the truth and be fair to us unless we do the same to others. You know how we talked about setting a boundary and following through with a consequence when someone crosses that line? Well, having good boundaries also means you need to follow through on your promises and commitments.

In life, in friendships and particularly in school, we make a lot of commitments. And when you have good boundaries, you respect other people's needs and fulfil your commitments. Yes, that means doing your share of that group project and actually getting your homework done. Yes, even if it's boring! Yes, even if you are scared of getting bad marks! You won't know until you submit it.

One of the best things you can try to be is a reliable person. When you have bad boundaries, you make promises you can't keep, or you back out of plans that you make, and as a result, people might struggle to trust you. You may not even trust yourself. How many times have you promised yourself things and not followed through? Well, it's time for that to end!

In every group project, there's often someone who doesn't do their share of work or doesn't show up when they say they will, or who says they will do something and then ALWAYS forgets. These people are not treating everyone else's time with respect and are not honouring their commitments.

Have you ever made a promise you knew you couldn't keep? Maybe you promised your teacher that you would do your homework, even though you knew you had lots of clubs after school and wouldn't have time? Maybe you promised three different friends that you would have lunch with them and realized you couldn't possibly keep your promise to them all? It can be really tempting to make up a lie in these instances to stop yourself getting in trouble with teachers, parents or friends. 'White lies' are small lies you tell to avoid hurting someone's feelings. The problem is that telling white lies is a sign of having bad boundaries and even if you have good intentions, honesty is always the best policy! If you get in the habit of telling white lies, then people will struggle to trust you. A white lie is still a lie.

Honesty is the best policy!

We are going to become good at following through on everything we say. When you respect someone, you respect their time. When you respect someone, you are honest with them, even if it might disappoint them.

No to white lies!
No to being late!
No to missing deadlines!
No to saying yes to things you know you won't do!

But no one is being reliable with ME!

Let's be honest: not everyone is an expert boundary-setter (like you will be after reading this book!). And that can be a difficult thing to deal with. Think back to that example of being lumped in a group with someone who doesn't do their share of the work.

What's the best thing to do in that situation? Do you do their work for them, or refuse to do it but then everyone gets a lower grade? When I was a people-pleaser, I would do everyone's work for them. All they had to do was ask, and if I'm being honest, sometimes they didn't even need to ask – I would just offer! I thought I was 'helping', but now I realize I wasn't helping them or myself, and I was doing a job that wasn't mine. Setting good boundaries involves knowing what is your responsibility and what is not. When you are a people-pleaser, you go above and beyond to get others to like you and that means you often put more on your plate than you should, whether that's feeling responsible for your parents' feelings or your friends' emotions or doing someone's work for them. Do that for the rest of your life and you are going to be exhausted!

Can you imagine being an adult, and agreeing to take on a second job, just because your colleague refuses to do theirs? But they get the salary for the work you've done! Totally unfair. So let's not get into the habit of taking on other people's jobs now. It's not up to you to do someone else's work, in the same way it's not up to you to look after someone else's emotions or handle someone else's arguments.

When we have clear boundaries, we know the line between ourselves and others. We know what belongs to us, whether it's our possessions, our emotions or our work, and we know we cannot control what doesn't belong to us. Other people's problems are their business, and your job is to focus on **your** business. Of course you can help people if they ask, but there is a difference between helping someone and doing everything for them. If you do their work for them, they will never learn how to do it themselves. **they** don't want that, **you** don't want that, and your teacher especially doesn't want that! You don't have to perform every task for every person. You don't have to say yes just because someone asks you, or even begs you.

You are allowed to say no!

As long as you are pulling your weight, it's OK to ask your peers to put their work in too. Here's how you can do this:

'We have all done our part and it's your turn to do your share.' Or: *'If you are struggling to get your part done, then ask for help but it's not OK to just not do anything.'*

And if they are still not listening, then you can ask the teacher if group work can actually be marked for your individual contributions. They might say no but you don't know until you ask – and asking is better than assuming. If they say no, then you can set a firm consequence for your group member:

'It's not cool to let down the whole team. If you don't want to be a part of the team, then we'll do our presentation without you.'

Your work is good enough, and so are you!

Sometimes we put off doing our work because we don't feel confident in ourselves or our abilities. So it feels easier to avoid rather than confront those feelings – feelings that might be telling you that you are stupid or useless or lazy or will never understand anything. You are none of these things. And you are especially **not** stupid! No one is stupid.

Some people are lucky and are naturally good at stuff without seeming to have to try as hard. And while being naturally good at something makes life easier, that doesn't mean you should give up if you don't get it straight away. For example, I was never good at English but I worked really hard at it and I ended up getting A* at GCSE. I was prouder of my A* in English than the A* I got in maths because I knew how much harder I had to work to get it in a subject that didn't come naturally to me.

We are all different and we all have different strengths. Some people are more skilled in sport or music or art, and when you become an adult, you can choose to put more time and energy into the things you like best. But you won't know what you want to pursue if you haven't tried everything with all your energy first. So for now, you should try your hardest at whatever you're doing, in order to give yourself the best shot at finding your skill and your passion and succeeding! And the way to do that is to stop being scared of getting things wrong.

Part of being a people-pleaser is the fear of getting things wrong. People-pleasers worry that if they make a mistake, it makes them a bad person. If you want to be a person with healthy boundaries, you need to know your 'goodness' doesn't depend on how many answers you get right. It's OK to try and not get it right; it doesn't mean you failed, it means you are learning – the point of learning is that you are discovering something new! The people-pleaser in us can tempt us into missing deadlines and delaying handing in our homework because we worry it's not good enough. The truth is, even if you get a bad mark, that doesn't make you a bad person. All you can do is try your best and submit your work with pride.

You don't need to tell your friends your grades!

It can be very tempting to compare yourself to your friends at school. There's nothing worse than coming out of an exam and everyone is sharing answers with each other, and you keep overhearing answers that you know you didn't write down! Whenever this happened to me, I would always feel so bad about myself. What I wish I knew then is that I didn't need to stick around and listen to it, and I definitely didn't need to tell anyone what I had written down. The exam was done! I couldn't change my answers! All I could do at that point was forget about the exam and celebrate all the hard work being over. Many years later, I realized that you can actually set boundaries around how you talk about your work.

I remember deciding not to tell people when I had an offer from a publisher to publish my first book. I didn't want to hear anyone else's opinions and I was worried that people might ruin the good news and the joy that it was bringing me. So at first I told no one! Then once I'd had a chance to celebrate myself, I started telling a few more people, and then a few more. I told people in stages, depending on how much I trusted them to keep it a secret and how much I knew they would celebrate with me. That meant the people who I told last were the ones who I thought might say something negative. And I never showed anyone my writing (apart from my agent and editor) until it was printed, out in the world and too late to change! This was the greatest boundary of them all. I would have never finished writing the book if I had had everyone else's opinions muddling my thoughts, so I put a boundary up and protected my work.

You can do that too!

You don't have to share information about your work with anyone. If you would rather just the teacher see it, then that's OK. And if you don't want to share your grades with anyone, then that's OK too.

And if there's one thing I want you to take from this chapter then it's this: if you get your results and they aren't as high as you would have liked . . . just remember that **grades don't define you**. By building boundaries around schoolwork, we can do our best AND submit on time, AND realize that grades, like any other number, cannot measure how amazing you are!

My time is precious!

Life can get really busy sometimes. Between school, homework and after-school stuff, it can sometimes feel like you are out of control of your own time! How do you push the stop button to just get a moment to breathe? I think you'll know the answer to this one, but . . . boundaries!

Our busy lives can often feel like we've left too many tabs open on our computer. We need to learn how to shut down some tabs, even if we know we have to reopen some at a later point. Having boundaries around our time means we can have more control over how we spend our day and prevent deadlines and our busy schedules from overwhelming us. We need to be able to say **no** to some things and **not now** to other things.

You want to know the top-secret way all the important people, like your head teacher, or even the prime minister, juggle their time? They know how to **prioritize** what needs to be done right now and what can wait. The first trick to meeting all your deadlines and getting everything done is ordering tasks from most to least important. The most important could be the one due first, or the one that is going to take the longest, or the one you find the hardest and need to dedicate the most time to. You are the captain and you get to decide what should be top of your agenda!

The next trick is to write a list. My favourite way to get everything done on time is to write a long to-do list. There is such satisfaction that comes from crossing things off that list and watching it get smaller. You get an amazing confidence boost knowing how productive you are being! And the best part is when you know you're on top of your to-do list, you can enjoy your relaxation time. We sometimes have to do boring things in life and yes, homework needs to get done. Isn't scrolling on TikTok more fun without the guilt of knowing you are missing your deadline? So, get it done and then have fun!

You need free time too!

The other key to having boundaries on your time is actually saying no to stuff. No matter how good you are at juggling all the things on your to-do list, you will start to feel exhausted if you can't say no to other things. If our to-do list is already too long, then we really need to pause before adding to it. Unfortunately, because you can't remove homework from your list, sometimes it means saying no to other things that sound like they'll probably be more fun. But nothing is that much fun if you're too burnt out to enjoy it!

It's important to make time for ourselves as part of our daily routine. Just like how we make time to eat every day, we need to make time to look after ourselves! We won't have the energy to do hard work or even enjoy time with our friends if we don't also have time to chill. Sometimes it's hard to create time for relaxation as a young person, because if you are caught relaxing for even a moment . . . well, cue all the moans about kids always being on their screens! And the same goes for when we aren't feeling well. No one should be forced to do somehthing when they're sick, whether you're a child going to school or an adult going to work.

The strongest of humans listen to their bodies and know the importance of giving their body and mind time to relax, switch off and recover.

Your body needs to be taken care of!

Work hard, play hard

When it comes to relaxing, everyone does this in different ways, so it's important to figure out what works best for you. And you need time to both play and rest – they aren't the same thing! Playing and resting meet different needs and fulfil a different part of your happiness. They are equally as important as hard work. Here are some of my top favourite ways to rest and play:

Rest

Watching TV

Meditating

Reading a book

Having a bath

Play

Playing a board game

Playing a game of squash

Painting

Paddleboarding

The ultimate form of rest is sleep, and a good night's sleep is important if you want to be full of energy the next day. But that's not the only type of rest we need. We need pauses and breaks in our day when our brain can wind down, and we can be a little quieter and slow down even for fifteen minutes. People need breaks! It's like if you are constantly walking on a treadmill, your legs will get tired. If you sit down after exercising for a while and let your body have a rest, when you go back to walking on the treadmill, you'll feel far more energetic and ready to continue moving. Our brains work the same way!

We don't need to be busy all the time! We all need to rest and more importantly, we all **deserve** to rest. You might feel like you are being lazy when you are doing nothing, but we have to remember that our time is exactly that: ours! And just because you are using it to relax, it doesn't mean it is a less productive use of time. Getting some well-earned rest is **never** a waste of time.

Next comes play! Just like how playtime is scheduled at school, we all need more playtime in life. Play fulfils the brain in a different way to rest. It creates more balance between work and distracts your mind and hands. My favourite way to play is with people, and this is a brilliant way to bond. Board games bring me so much joy, and more recently my boyfriend introduced me to how much fun video games are. Sometimes adults get annoyed at you when you use video games to play or rest. But as long as you aren't spending too long playing, and as long as you've prioritized your work and your other commitments, here's what you can say back:

'I know it looks like I'm not doing anything but I'm actually resting, and I have learned that's important for a balanced life.'

Who wants a life that has no room for fun? Definitely not me!

Now I'd like you to think about things that you want to make more time for in your life. Let's create a list of your favourite ways to rest and play and make sure you create some time for both this week!

Pick one of each and add them to your to-do list for the week. Then, watch how much more you enjoy looking at everything you've got planned over the next few days. Setting boundaries with your time and making time for **you** gives you things to look forward to and gives you more energy, joy and hope for the rest of the week!

Having fun is never a waste of time!

Ten rules for boundaries with your school

1. *It's not OK to yell at anyone*

2. *Teachers aren't always right . . .
   and you aren't either*

3. *If you commit to something,
   you have to follow through*

4. *You can't do everything and be
   everywhere all at once*

5. *When it comes to homework, you can
   only do your best and that's enough*

6. *Making time for rest is just as
   important as making time for work*

7. *Don't have to compare your grades to
   your friends' if you don't want to*

8. *Treat teachers with the same respect
   you want them to have for you*

9. *Good boundaries means following
   through on all commitments —
   from plans to projects to homework*

10. *If you are having a tough time with
    a teacher, ask an adult for help*

Chapter 5
No, this is my body

- How do I tell a someone to stop hugging me?

- How do I say no to a kiss?

- What if I'm not sure if I want to say yes or no?

- Am I weird because I'm not interested in love?

- Do I have to kiss someone to fit in?

Your body belongs to you, and you get to set your own rules. You get to decide if someone touches you, you get to decide if you want more personal space and you can absolutely say NO when someone is invading your physical boundaries. Everyone has different boundaries when it comes to their body, and that makes sense because everybody is different! Sometimes your boundaries might change and that's totally OK. Consent is a really important topic to explore, so let's talk about saying no to people who try to break your bodily boundaries.

I don't do hugs

Remember how I said boundaries are like an invisible bubble around you, protecting you from the outside? Well, that bubble also exists to protect your body and your personal space. Just like our skin is a barrier that protects us from the outside world, we need our boundaries to protect us too.

Have you ever been in a crowd where there is no room and it's so uncomfortable because all these people are so close to you that you can nearly smell what they had for breakfast? This is uncomfortable for many reasons. You might feel squashed. Or suffocated. Or frustrated. Or perhaps you feel that your personal space is being invaded. And you don't need to be in a huge crowd to feel this way. It can feel the same if someone is standing a little too close to you when having a conversation. There are lots of things you might want to say no to when thinking about your bodily and physical boundaries:

No to someone invading your personal space!

No to someone touching your body without permission!

No to someone crossing your physical boundaries!

What is consent?

Consent is a word we hear all the time, but what does it actually mean?

Consent: Permission or agreement to have something happen or to do something.

Consent might seem like a big word, but you already ask for consent every day! It's when you ask a friend if you can come over to their house, or you ask your sibling if they want to play a game with you. It doesn't have to be a long conversation or a scary decision to bring up the topic of consent. It can just be you asking before you give someone a hug. Or you saying no when someone wants to touch you in a way that you are not comfortable with. It's you saying no to the space invaders! A smart man called John Oliver once said:

'[consent] is like boxing. If one person does not agree to it, then you are committing a crime.'

If two people agree, then you have yourself a boxing match. But if one person doesn't want to play, and it's just them being punched by another person – that's when there's a problem!

Consent is especially important when it comes to our bodies, particularly the private parts. You know what I mean by these parts – breasts, penises, vulvas, vaginas. The parts that are usually hidden by clothes. When you are older you might allow people to touch you there, but that should only happen when the other person has your permission and you trust them. If someone ever touches your body in *any* area that makes you uncomfortable, then it's important to tell them to stop and then go tell an adult you trust. No one is allowed to make you feel uncomfortable in your own body. When you say no and tell an adult, you are protecting your boundaries and keeping yourself safe.

You don't have to hug to say hi!

Everyone is different when it comes to physical boundaries. Some people will want a big bubble around them and a lot of distance, and some people only need a little space. This can also vary depending on who you're speaking to and how well you know the person. My best friends could koala-bear hug me and I would have no issue, whereas it will take me some time to feel comfortable with newbies in my life getting that close to me. You might love it when your sister gets in your bed for a chat, but if your cousin did that – awkward! You might share an ice cream with your friends all the time, but if you find out that your brother has used your toothbrush – YUCK! That is NOT the same! You might not mind a kiss on the cheek from your godfather, but when some random family friend whose name you don't even know does it, your brain just screams **INVASION! ABORT!**

When you're speaking to someone, think about where you want your bubble to be. If you decide someone is stepping into your bubble, you can always step back, and if they keep getting closer then you could ask them to maintain the space between you with comments such as:

- **'I just like my own space. Thanks for respecting that!'**

- **'I need a bit of space to breathe.'**

- **'I can hear you where you are.'**

- **'Can you still hear me? I can speak up, rather than us standing any closer.'**

Your invisible bubble is there to keep you safe and make you feel comfortable. You are allowed to protect your space! I don't know about you, but I find my personal space is encroached on the most at big events where there are friends and family, and extended family, and those friends of the family who you tend to only see once a year. My family are not huggers so when family friends I barely know do it, I feel uncomfortable. If I can't remember the last time I hugged my brother, then I am not going to want to hug a pal of my dad's who I haven't seen since the last big event! Having a hug forced upon me is the WORST!

It's your body, so if you say no to someone hugging you, then that deserves to be respected. Some people love hugs. And some people don't. We are all different, and if hugs are not your thing, then you have other options. Handshake, high five or wave at a distance – these are all acceptable ways of greeting people that require less or no contact. You need to figure out what works best for you to be able to tell people what you want. Why don't you start trying out these different ways of greeting people and figure out what makes you feel most comfortable. This way, going forward, you'll be able to set very clear boundaries round your physical space:

- **Wave**

- **Handshake**

- **High five**

- **Fist bump**

- **Hug**

Although you do need to bear in mind that the other person will have their own preferences too. If they tell you a certain greeting makes them uncomfortable, you must respect that.

Once you've decided which ones make you feel most comfortable, you can make sure that this becomes the way people greet you. When it comes to greeting people, the most confident approach tends to win. That doesn't mean go in with a chest bump or a thumb war! What I mean by this is that if you and a cousin are approaching each other and she wants a hug but you want a handshake, the person who goes in the most confidently with their greeting will tend to come out on top. So waving your hand quickly and firmly is an easy way to send a message that you'd rather not hug. Be confident in whichever greeting you choose and present it to the other person as if that's the only option.

But if you don't get there in time, and someone goes in first for a hug, this is when you can use your voice. You are allowed to communicate your discomfort and ask that people respect your boundaries. Here's how you say no:

'Hugs aren't my thing; how about a high five?'

Or:

'I'm not a hugger – how about a handshake?'

If someone lands a hug on you without you seeing it coming, then you can voice your discomfort too:

'Oh, I didn't expect that. Can you ask before you hug me next time?'

Or:

'This is making me feel uncomfortable. I need you to stop touching me.'

I know that these sentences can sound quite firm, especially if you are not used to standing up for yourself, but you are allowed to be firm when people cross your body boundaries. And it only feels weird because you haven't used the words before! It's always scary before you try something new and therefore speaking up will feel strange. But when someone crosses your physical boundaries, that's when your biggest NO needs to be used. It doesn't matter what that person thinks of you – it matters that you feel safe.

Your safety is your top priority!

No is not a rude word!

You know how I said earlier that my family are not huggers? Well, it makes it even weirder that when I was younger, I was often told I was being rude if I didn't go around the room and greet everyone at family events. I would often be told to 'go give your uncle a hug' or 'go give your auntie a kiss'. But you do not need to hug and kiss people you don't want to in order to be polite.

Even though boundaries are so important, people only started speaking openly about them relatively recently. This means that lots of adults were never taught that it's OK to say no to forced hugs and greetings and gestures, or to discover what they find most comfortable. So when they say you're being rude, it's likely because they were never taught that they can say no to these things themselves.

Your body belongs to you, and you get to set your own rules. Ignoring your own needs in order to 'be polite' means you're not listening to how you're feeling. It is more important that you are comfortable than that you are considered polite. If they want to think you are rude, then let them. As long as you've explained your boundaries clearly and fairly, you can move forward confidently knowing you are doing nothing wrong.

Just because it helps you, doesn't mean it helps them!

As I said before, you might have different boundaries for different people, but did you also know you could have different boundaries at different times? For example, although I don't enjoy hugging people I barely know, I do love big hugs with people I'm close with. But if I'm angry, I don't want anyone to touch me. I need my space, and only once I've processed my anger do I feel comfortable with other people touching me. I get it – when someone is angry or upset, you might assume that a hug will make them feel better, so you reach over to go comfort them. It's a nice gesture! But it's always better to not assume. Just because a hug would make you feel better doesn't mean it will make others feel better. What's the solution? Ask! *'Would you like a hug?'*

You are giving the person the chance to say no and to tell you what they want. Who knows? They might actually want space and that could be what makes them feel better. And now when I want a hug and no one is giving me one, instead of getting sad, I know I need to ask for one because maybe THEY don't know that's what would help me. *'Can you give me a hug?'*

When you get in the habit of asking instead of assuming, what you are actually doing is getting consent and asking that person to let you know how you can help them. You can ask this more directly if you like as well: *'Is there anything I can do to help and support you in this moment?'*

Consent, even in these small moments, is the best way to make sure everyone is comfortable.

Remember: your body, your rules!

Your first kiss

I was the last of all my friends to have my first kiss. It was on the second day of university when I was eighteen years old. I worried so much about kissing! How do you actually do it? Where do you put your hands? Where does your tongue go? Does it feel the same as kissing the back of your hand? What if I've just eaten food and my breath stinks? Do they ask before they kiss you? I also felt really insecure about the fact that I was later than all my friends to have that experience. If you asked me at the time, I actually had no interest in kissing someone and if I'm being really honest, the only reasons I did were:

- I didn't want to be left out.

- I didn't want to be considered weird.

- I didn't want to be judged for it.

Looking back, they don't sound like very good reasons to kiss someone. But at the time I wrongly believed that if you hadn't kissed someone by eighteen years old, then it said a number of things about you. I thought it meant you weren't pretty enough, cool enough or popular enough. What I wish I knew at the time was:

You are allowed to wait until you are ready.

To me, kissing felt like such a pivotal part of growing up, and it also felt like it was part of a checklist I hadn't been able to tick off. I actually ended up lying to all my friends at the age of sixteen and pretending I'd kissed someone, because I worried that they wouldn't want to stay friends with me otherwise.

But no one should ever feel pressured into lowering their boundaries. If anyone does this to you, they are not a good friend. A true friend will encourage you to wait until you are ready and when you do finally have that kiss, they won't make a big deal out of it. Or they might, but in a good way because they are excited for you!

If not kissing someone is a reason someone doesn't like you, **let them not like you**. We should never convince someone to like us by doing something that makes us uncomfortable. It is no one else's business when you kiss someone for the first time, and it shouldn't have to be public knowledge when you do. You are allowed your privacy and you are allowed to say:

'I don't want to talk about this. Let's end this conversation and talk about something else!'

If you are not ready to kiss, take your time. Everyone is allowed to live life at their own speed and if someone goes in to kiss you, and you aren't ready, that's all you have to say.

'No – I'm not ready for that.'

If you change your mind, you can let them know, but make sure you are doing what *you* want to do, not what someone is persuading or pressuring you to do. If you say no, and someone keeps pressuring you into doing it, it is called **coercion**.

Coercion: Persuading someone to do something they are not comfortable with by pressuring them, threatening them or forcing them.

This could be someone saying 'I'll tell everyone you're weird if you don't kiss me', or 'I'm going to tell everyone you kissed me anyway so you might as well'. These are people who don't deserve your kisses.

It is important that the person you kiss is someone who will accept your FIRST no. A no should not be an invitation for someone to keep trying. When you say no, the other person should accept what you have said and give you space. If they are not willing to wait, then it's a good thing that you know sooner rather than later. You don't want to be with someone simply because of this intimate part of the relationship. You want to be able to chat together, have fun without kissing and enjoy spending time with each other without the pressure of doing things that you don't want to do.

If they are a good person and accept your no the first time, but you want them to know that you are still interested in them, you can tell them:

'I still like you. I just need you to be more patient.' Or: *'I need more time to get to know you. Can we take things a little bit slower?'*

If you start kissing and you change your mind, you can also tell them to stop. Listen to your feelings. Listen to your body and remember that you don't have to explain yourself. The fact that you don't want to any more is reason enough to stop. You don't need to feel guilty for saying no and you don't need to feel guilty for changing your mind. Your answer could have been yes a minute ago and now it's a no. The person you kiss should still be kind whether it's a yes or a no, and if their kindness depends on a certain answer, then that's not a person who deserves your kisses!

Once I had kissed someone, I realized it wasn't as important as everyone made it out to be! Your first kiss is simply that . . . your first. So it doesn't need to be perfect or your best. After all, it's hard for your first kiss to be your best because you've never done it before. It would be like trying to be an Olympic swimmer the first time you get into a pool!

If it's not a hell yes, it's a no!

This is just going to be a short section of this chapter, but arguably the most important. As we covered in the last section, no means no. Especially when it comes to your body, consent and people touching you. If you ever say no, it doesn't mean 'convince me'. It doesn't mean 'try harder'. And it doesn't mean 'I actually mean yes'. It means no. Plain and simple . . . or is it?

I want to talk to you about something called **enthusiastic consent**. The idea of enthusiastic consent is all about that difference between someone not saying no, and someone actively saying yes. It's about raising the bar from something that feels just OK to something that feels more than OK.

To work out what feels good to you, and to determine if there's something that you want to enthusiastically consent to, you need to check in with your feelings. Feelings can be confusing, though, and can take a bit of time to understand. Sometimes your feelings can be overwhelming and it's hard to sort them out in your brain. That's OK!

Your emotions are your body's way of telling you what's going on inside you. This top-secret information is reserved for the Very Important People . . . or I should say, one Very Important Person: you! Because you don't need to share it with anyone if you don't want to. You know how cars have a flashing light that tells you when the petrol is low? From the outside, the car looks like a normal car, but if you are on the inside, the flashing light tells you something is wrong. In the same way, if you're in a situation and you get that little warning light of emotions telling you something isn't quite right, remember this: **If it's not a hell yes, it's a no!**

Why is this sentence better? Because you *know* when it's a **'HELL YES!'** You don't have to pause or think or question. You can feel that yes in your bones and you are 100 per cent certain it's a yes because it feels good to say yes. It feels right to say yes. If it's anything less than that, then it's a no. Even if you are only feeling a little unsure. Even if you have that iffy feeling in your stomach and your brain keeps questioning what to do. If your warning light is flashing, that means you need to slow down and not rush into a decision right now.

It can sometimes be hard to know how you feel in an exact moment. I often wonder how other people think and speak so quickly, as sometimes it takes a while for my feelings to catch up with my brain and then my brain to figure out what to say. It's why, throughout the book, I've given you sentences to say in certain situations, to save you some 'figuring out' time. Hopefully, one of those handy phrases can pop into your brain and help you out. Here are some more:

'I am not comfortable with that and I need you to stop touching me.'

And: *'I've asked you to stop. Please respect my wishes.'*

What I want you to know is that you don't need a fancy sentence, your no is enough. No is a full sentence. Even if you can't find any other words in that moment, use your **no**.

Use it often and use it firmly.

No more apologizing for our boundaries!

No more pretending we are comfortable when we aren't!

No more making everyone happy at our own expense!

Ten rules for boundaries around your body

1. **You don't have to hug anyone you don't want to**

2. **Respect other people's personal space**

3. **If someone is making you feel uncomfortable, say something**

4. **You are not rude for declining physical touch**

5. **You are allowed to have different body boundaries to other people**

6. **Ask for consent before you touch someone's body**

7. **You get to decide how you greet people**

8. **You not wanting to do something is a big enough reason to say no**

9. **You should never have to kiss someone to get them to like you**

10. **You can change your mind and withdraw consent whenever you want**

Chapter 6
No, this is me

- How can I feel more confident wearing whatever I want?

- What do I say if someone is mean about the way I look?

- Why don't I look like my friends?

- How can I feel better about the way I look?

- How do I say 'no' to following the crowd?

As we get older, we might become interested in experimenting with self-expression, discovering who we really are, and exploring our identity. You might want to try out new hairstyles or new clothes, and you might find yourself playing around, having fun and changing your mind over and over again. Other people might tell you that you need to look a certain way, but no, no, NO! You are uniquely you and no one should tell you how to look, dress or be.

The world is my catwalk

You know those days in school when you are allowed to wear your own clothes? I think it's supposed to be fun, but often it's really not. Sometimes you spend weeks planning your outfit and still worry that it's not cool enough! Do you secretly want to dye your hair a crazy colour or personalize your jeans, but you're scared of being judged? Well, I'm here to tell you that no one ever started a new fashion trend by blending in. You were born to stand out and your self-expression matters!

On the other days, you are stuck with your uniform, and although that makes it easier in the morning because you don't have to think about what you are wearing, I know it can feel hard to find your own style and express yourself when you are all wearing the same uniform. The same way flowers are all beautiful and look different, so do humans. And whether you

get given a bunch of roses or daffodils or tulips or daisies, they all look wonderful individually and wonderful together because all flowers are special and beautiful in their own way!

Have you ever heard that beauty is in the eye of the beholder? Well, it's true! Have you ever gone to an art museum and wondered how can THAT be called art? It's just a black line on a piece of white paper. Well, to someone else that is a gorgeous and powerful piece of art . . . but to you, well, you just don't get it. And that's OK.

The same is true for clothes and fashion – what is beautiful to you might not be to someone else. But that doesn't and shouldn't matter.

Choosing how you look and dress is an amazing way to express yourself. And the key to all of it is knowing that you are not allowed to express a negative opinion about what anyone is wearing, and equally, they are not allowed to express a negative opinion about what you are wearing. When someone offers you up an opinion on what you are wearing that you didn't ask for, guess what you should say back? NO.

'I didn't ask for your opinion, so I would appreciate it if you kept it to yourself.'

'Well, I love my outfit – it makes me happy and that's all that matters!'

It's so much fun walking through the world like you are in a fashion show and the pavement is your catwalk. And the trick is that you have to own what you are wearing! Can you imagine if models were hunched and embarrassed when they walked down the catwalk? It would look weird! But when they walk

with confidence, no matter how odd their outfit is (and let's be honest, some outfits at fashion shows can be a bit strange!), it's suddenly the new cool thing. And that's because they are walking around with confidence.

It's your job to see your beauty!

When I was in school, I looked different to all my friends. I thought looking different meant I wasn't beautiful; I even sometimes thought I was ugly. I am mixed race, I have scars on my stomach and I am fat. I wish I had known at the time that there is a difference between being beautiful and fitting the **'beauty ideal'**.

There are some massive industries that try to sell us one version of beauty – this is called the beauty ideal. The beauty ideal is the picture of beauty that you see the most, whether that's on social media, magazines, on fashion catwalks or on the TV. This then filters down into everyday life, so the people in school who are seen as the most pretty tend to be people who, by chance, happen to look like the beauty ideal at that moment. The beauty ideal is constructed largely by the fashion, beauty and diet industries, which will tell you that you need to be thinner or taller or whatever else they deem 'trendy', in order to look good! And the goal is always for them to make money. So, for example, you might see companies advertising with lines like 'blondes have more fun'. But what if you aren't blonde? Do you really have to become blonde to be fun? No, of course not! But if they sell the lie that changing your hair colour can increase the fun in your life, they can then watch on from afar as all their blonde hair dye flies off the shelf and makes them more money!

The beauty ideal is constantly changing.

As a result, it becomes impossible to always fit it. One day, straight hair will be in, and off you go to buy some straighteners. Then a few weeks later, it's all about beach waves, and away the straighteners go and out come the curling wands. These businesses want to make you feel bad about how you look because it means they can sell you products and make money off your insecurity. If you already believe you are beautiful, though, then they can't keep taking your money!

Think about it . . . if they tell you your teeth are yellow, you might buy tooth-whitening products. Because if they tell you that your teeth are perfect the colour they are, there is nothing to sell. If companies tell you that flawless skin is beautiful, you will buy skin creams to hide blemishes and make-up to cover spots. If they were to tell you that spots are normal and they're nothing to be embarrassed about, then they lose money!

I was never even close to the beauty ideal, but that didn't mean I wasn't beautiful! When I was growing up, the beauty ideal was to be as thin as possible. There was a phrase people would ask: 'Does my bum look big in this?' – and they would always want the answer to be no! But then suddenly, the trend changed, and it became really popular to have a big bum. Overnight, the beauty ideal shifted its idea of what is beautiful and all that time we'd spent worrying about whether our bum looked too big didn't matter any more! This is why we can't base our opinions on what the beauty ideal says. You have to remember that other people's opinion are not as important as your own.

I am still mixed race. I still have scars on my stomach. I am still fat. And I still believe I'm beautiful. You know why? Because I see my beauty! I see the beauty when I smile and my eyes scrunch up like my Chinese mum's eyes. And I love that I have bushy eyebrows like my Jewish dad. I love that I look different and all the differences I worried about when I was younger are things that make me special. I know sometimes it's hard to love what you look like all the time, but you need to **accept** what you look like. You've only been given one face and one body, and you are going to spend a lot of time together. Sometimes we are so hard on our bodies, but we have to remember that we are on the same team.

If you can't see your own beauty, then why should anyone else?

If you aren't going to be nice to yourself, then why should anyone else?

Let's take some time today to notice the beautiful things about ourselves! Bonus points if you discover something that you've never spotted before – like a freckle on your nose. Look in the mirror and any time a negative thought pops into your head, I want you to come up with two positive things. Then, take a step back and look at yourself as a whole. Sometimes when we are focusing on the things we don't like, we are looking at our face or a specific body part too closely. It's a lot easier to see the good when you are taking in the full picture!

Remember how I said that boundaries are about teaching people how you want to be treated? Well, that means you need to lead by example. You have to treat yourself the best way you possibly can, and then other people will do the same. It is your job to be kind to yourself and when that nasty inner critic pipes up, I want you to say to it: **'No. I don't deserve this.'**

What you feel is more important than what you look like

I believe the key to accepting what you look like is realizing that it actually doesn't matter as much as how you feel. For instance, do you worry in PE lessons that you look silly attempting to do the exercises? Start focusing on how you are feeling and how much *fun* you are having, and you might find that the worries about how you look start to disappear.

Or if you are dancing and someone thinks you look silly? **Look silly!** Your job is not to look perfect every second of the day. Your job is to enjoy yourself and have fun!

You are more than just a body.

Your opinion is the only one that matters!

When I don't want to wear make-up, I don't. Even if all my friends are wearing make-up. I also really love dresses, so sometimes that means I turn up to really casual events in a flowy dress. I often get comments from people such as, 'Where are you going all dressed up?' and I just reply, 'Why save all my favourite dresses for special occasions? I don't need an occasion.' I dress myself how I want to dress myself and I set my own rules. When someone tells me they don't like what I am wearing, I say: 'No. I didn't ask for your opinion.'

Having good boundaries means caring more about what you think than about what other people think. And if you stick to what YOU like, you never know – you might end up setting some new trends yourself.

You can even show your friends how to be kinder to themselves too! The same way you are being your own bodyguard and protecting yourself from mean words, when you hear your friends saying mean things about themselves, you can be their bodyguard too. Whenever I hear my friends talking badly about themselves or the way they look, I say, 'Hey! That's my friend you are talking about. Don't talk to her like that!'

It helps them realize that we should never bully ourselves. We need to be kind to ourselves! **We need to take back the power!** Only we can decide what is beautiful and what is not.

One of the weird rules society has also created is around what girls and boys should look like. These are called gender stereotypes. Stereotypes are widely held beliefs that over-simplify things that should not be simplified. Such as gender! Gender is a lot more complicated than the idea that all boys like one thing and all girls like another. Who decided that girls like make-up and boys like sport?! We should all be able to pick and choose what we like instead of following some random rules. From clothes to make-up to hobbies, nothing should be off limits to anyone based on their gender. Everyone should have permission to experiment with and discover their own interests. **Be a rule breaker!**

It's time to say 'get lost' to the beauty ideals and pressure from society that says you have to look or be a certain way. We don't have to fit into one narrow version of the beauty ideal or gender stereotypes. We can all be different in our own way and still all be beautiful. And most of all, being beautiful is not the most important thing in the world. It's much more important to be happy and kind to yourself and others. If anyone tries to tell you that you have to change who you are or the way you look, then I want you to say:

NO,

NO,

NO!

Defend your body

Having a body that is constantly changing is a minefield to navigate, especially while trying to keep your self-esteem intact. Eurghhh . . . doesn't growing up suck? You have just got on board with your body, worked hard to accept how it looks, and then it goes and changes! It brings aches and pains and hair in strange places and things that you have to figure out (such as periods!). You either feel left behind or too far ahead and, well, change is always difficult. It's a tough time, so you need to make sure that you are saying nice things to yourself. You have to become your body's best friend. If you don't, no one else will!

It never made sense to me when people spoke badly about their bodies, because they usually spoke about the thing that they never wanted people to notice. Imagine if you had a friend who was really self-conscious about his elbows. To you they look totally normal, but to him, they're WEIRD! Now what do you think people will do every time he mentions his weird elbows? Look at them – of course!

When I was first trained as a life coach, I learned that everyone has an insecurity. I solely worked with people who had body-image issues and they all had a story of someone making a comment or saying something mean that created their insecurity. They had let someone else's opinion inside and this had affected how they viewed their own body. We can't let that happen! We cannot ever agree with the bullies! And you definitely can't join them. Sometimes we make jokes about our body before other people make them because then it feels like we are in on the joke and they can't hurt us. Actually, it means that you become your own bully. When you make the joke first, remember your body can hear you! The other person doesn't have to live in your body every day, but you do! So it hurts more when you make these comments yourself, because you and your body have been through so much together and have a special relationship that no one else is part of. We have to be our body's best protector.

Say no to unsolicited opinions about the way you look!

Say no to turning against your own body!

Say no to body shaming!

What is body shaming?

Body shaming is when someone makes you feel bad about your appearance. It could be them saying that they don't like how you look, telling you to change your body or insulting you with words such as 'ugly'. It's when someone shames you for what you look like. Body shame could be comments about your weight, your hair or anything about your appearance. It's particularly mean because we don't get to choose the body we're born in. Can you imagine if we were only nice to people who wore size 5 shoes? It would be so odd, wouldn't it? So why do we seem to feel differently about people's body shape and size? If we can accept that feet can range from a size 1 to size 22, then we should accept that bodies can differ just as much!

Body shaming is not acceptable . . . ever!

If someone says something unkind about the way you look, it can leave a mark on you for a long time. It's perfectly normal to feel hurt by these comments, and if you do find that someone is trying to body shame you, you can set a strong boundary:

'Please stop commenting on my body.'

If someone continues to talk negatively about your body, then you have three options: an easy, medium and advanced option. I want you to work up to the advanced option, as I understand that might seem impossible right now.

Easy option: Excuse yourself from the conversation. Say you are going to go in the other room to get some food or drink, or that you are going to the toilet. State a reason to leave the conversation and don't come back until they are talking about a different topic – a topic that isn't your body!

Medium option: No more joining in on the body shame. Stay silent. Yes, completely silent. Silence makes people awkward, and they should feel awkward! It's really hard to keep having a conversation with someone who is silent, so they will get the message faster than if you fight back or even try to justify the way your body looks. You don't need to explain your body to them, anyway!

Advanced option: This is my favourite option and the only one I use. When people talk about my body, I ask them to stop. If they continue, then I say:

185

'I have asked you once to stop talking about my body. I am not going to stay in this conversation to be insulted, so I'm going to leave the room and you can come find me when you are ready to talk about something else.'

Right now, it might feel like you will never be able to get to the advanced option, but trust me, you will get there. If a person is body shaming another, **they are always in the wrong.** And once you realize this, it becomes easy to be firm about it. We need to put an end to all body shame.

Families can body shame too!

Sometimes body shaming even comes from our families. Unfortunately, adults have grown up in the same world as us and that means they might also think there is just one version of beauty. Often the people who body shame others are those who are not happy in their own bodies. Or sometimes the parents who body shame their children were body shamed by their parents when they were younger. Nonetheless, it can be really hurtful when it comes from the people you love most. I want you to know that if a parent body shames you, they are in the wrong. Just like you would ask a friend or stranger to stop, you can also tell your parents or family members to stop, and you can leave the room if they continue talking about your body. No one deserves to feel bad about their body and if your family don't have the tools to know how to accept their own bodies, perhaps you can start on that road together!

The key to unlocking your body confidence

I spent many years learning to love my body, and the good news is, if you work at setting boundaries and saying no to people knocking your confidence, the way you view your body actually changes . . . I would know! I used to be so insecure about what I look like, but now I wouldn't want my body to be any different than it is. I love my body wholeheartedly and I'm so thankful that this is the body that I've been given.

It all starts with appreciation and respect.

You don't have to love what you look like every second of the day, but you have to respect your body. Remember we spoke about respect? So how do you treat a person you respect? You are polite and kind to them. At the very least, you can appreciate your body for what it can do. Some bodies cannot do all the same things as other bodies, but it's important to remember that your body is unique to you and to celebrate what it **CAN** do.

Too often, we focus on the ways our bodies look different to others, but we rarely notice all the things that are great about them. Let's take a moment to do that now. Grab a pen and paper, and fill in the end of these sentences:

I love my body because.....

I love my body because.....

I love my body because.....

Our bodies are the best. We wouldn't be here without them! They do so much for us and don't ask for anything in return, so THE LEAST we can do is be kind to them! Part of what makes our bodies the best is that they are different! We aren't made from the same cookie cutter, like gingerbread men (why do we never talk about gingerbread women?). We all have different features, skin tones, we're different shapes and sizes, different genders, some people have disabilities, which can be visible or invisible . . . People who believe we should all be the same can be unkind about differences, but we have to remember that being different is not a bad thing. **It's wonderful because it means you are one of a kind!**

I have a lot of scars on my stomach and, when I was growing up, people weren't very kind about this. But no one in the world has a stomach like mine – how cool is that? And once I realized that, I started noticing how all the surgery scars on my stomach actually make up a smile. So if you see me wandering

by the pool in a bikini, you've got two smiles staring at you. One on my face and one on my tummy!

Your body might be changing right now and it can take a lot of work and time to adjust to all the newness. But by saying no to body shaming and learning to appreciate and respect your body, I'm confident that you will get there.

Your body is perfect the way it is, and you and your body are on the same team. Your body is your day-one bestie; it has literally been there for you since the beginning. So if anyone tries to get you to turn against it, tell them where your loyalties lie. If you aren't going to defend it, no one will.

No one deserves to feel bad about their body – no matter what they look like!

Ten rules for boundaries around your identity

1. **Your body is your business**

2. **Ask before giving your opinion**

3. **It's up to you to decide how you express yourself — and it's OK to change your mind**

4. **You can define beauty for yourself . . . and others don't have to agree**

5. **Body shaming is never acceptable**

6. **You don't have to care what people think**

7. **Be your own bodyguard**

8. **You and your body are on the same team!**

9. **You don't have to love your body, but you do need to respect and appreciate it**

10. **You are perfect as you are, and don't need to change for anyone**

Chapter 7
Start saying no

- Where do I start?

- What if I'm not strong enough?

- What's the first boundary to set?

- How do I know when enough is enough?

- How do I respond when someone else says no?

- What if someone doesn't accept my no?

Before we go our separate ways, I want to give you some final practical tips on how and when to say no. We are going to talk about how to know when your boundaries are crossed so you know when you need to do something about it. And we're going to talk about paying attention to your emotions, as they give you a HUGE clue to knowing when it's time to say NO. I hope this helps you go back out into the world feeling more confident and ready to set clear boundaries. Because you DESERVE to set the rules for your own life.

No way! No more! Not me! Not now!

We want to find the balance of saying no the right amount and at the right times. If we say no all the time, we end up making our world very small and might be cutting ourselves off from trying new and fun things because we are scared. But then . . . if you never say no, you'll be exhausted from living life on everyone else's terms; you will struggle to know how you really feel and people will walk all over you because you will never learn how to stand up for yourself.

So where's the middle ground? The middle ground is identifying your boundaries and saying no when they are crossed. And in order to know which boundaries are most important to you, you need to be in tune with your emotions. Emotions are really important for knowing how to communicate and set your boundaries. And the first thing I want you to do is forget everything you know about emotions!

We get taught a lot of confusing things about emotions because even the adults in our lives often don't know how to deal with them. It's not their fault really – it's not like there's a class in school labelled HOW TO DEAL WITH YOUR EMOTIONS. Wow, I wish there was though! Wait . . . let's do that.

Welcome to your emotion masterclass!

Rule 1: All emotions are good.

Sometimes we get told that emotions are bad or wrong because other people are uncomfortable with them. But the only reason they are uncomfortable is because when they were your age, they were never taught how powerful and important emotions can be.

Rule 2: Everyone has emotions!

Don't let anyone make fun of you for having emotions. It doesn't mean you are weak or too sensitive. And you aren't being dramatic! You are allowed to have your feelings hurt. Sometimes it can seem like the world wants you to walk around like a robot with no feelings, but if you listen to your emotions, they can be your superpower, and they are also hugely important in helping you set boundaries!

Rule 3: Thoughts create emotions . . . and sometimes our thoughts aren't telling the truth.

Did you know that for an emotion to exist, you have to have a thought first? Want proof? Let's try a quick experiment. Imagine biting into a lemon. Really imagine it. Is your mouth drooling? See, I told you! You thought about biting into a lemon and your body reacted to the sourness even though the lemon doesn't exist, because your unconscious mind doesn't know the difference between what you are imagining and what is real. This is what happens when you imagine something stressful or unpleasant, such as everyone hating you. Your body will start feeling stressed because it thinks this is true! This is why we have to be careful about our thoughts and which ones we are spending too much time focusing on.

Rule 4: Your feelings are important, even if no one understands!

Have you ever seen a toddler collapse into a puddle of tears over something small, such as their shoelace coming undone, and wondered why they are making such a big deal over nothing? It's not the end of the world! But it is to them: you have to remember that they are smaller, and their world is smaller too. Telling them in that moment that they are being silly or overreacting isn't going to help them. And no matter how much you ignore them, and no matter how silly it is to you, those feelings are real to them and that's actually all that matters! Your emotions are the same. Even if no one understands why something is impacting you in the way it does, your feelings are valid and important.

But what do emotions have to do with saying no? Everything! Emotions are designed to be temporary. If you listen to them and do what they are telling you to do, they are more likely to go away! So if someone crosses your boundaries and a negative emotion arises in you, if you set the boundary, the emotion will go POOF!

Anger and resentment: The secret weapon to knowing whether or not a boundary has been crossed!

Let's talk about anger! This very important emotion tells you that your boundaries are being crossed, and it fills you with energy. Have you ever been completely exhausted and then someone did something annoying, and you suddenly got VERY angry? You've gone from exhausted to full of energy in no time at all! The reason it gives you all this energy is that anger is designed to give you the power and strength to stand up for yourself. Anger is wonderful like that, but the reason it gets a bad reputation is because of what people do with that extra energy. Sometimes when people get that surge of energy, they don't know how to channel it into saying no and instead they do things such as get louder, scream, shout and become aggressive.

Emotions themselves are never wrong, but how you express them might be. The fact you are feeling angry is great because it means you know where your boundaries are, but yelling, screaming or getting physical towards others is never OK. Anger is not a reason to lose control of how you behave and remember what I told you . . . you always, *always* want to be proud of the way you behave! When you notice your anger arising, imagine it like the line on a bowling alley that alerts you when you step across it. That's all your anger is doing – it's letting you know that someone is crossing your boundary, and you can thank your anger for flagging this. Then, take a deep breath and decide what you want to do about it. My suggestion is to set a boundary!

The other emotion that will help you set boundaries is **resentment**. You will feel resentment in your body as a second warning when you ignore anger. This is the emotion that says, 'My boundary has been crossed and you are doing nothing about it!' The resentment occurs because you feel that what has taken place was unfair and, as you did nothing to protect yourself, the feeling is trapped within you. If we listen to our anger the first time, we are more likely to avoid reaching resentment. Resentment is our second chance. Resentment is an emotion that actually comes from the envy family. Yes, that green-eyed monster! We are envious of those who find setting boundaries and saying no easy. With resentment, as with anger, it's important that we are able to differentiate between the feeling in our bodies and how we act.

A warning sign that you might be feeling resentful is if you start making **passive-aggressive comments**. This could be making subtle digs about how someone never helps, or even calling someone lazy, rather than just asking them to help. We are annoyed but we aren't brave enough to talk about it, so it simmers inside us. The best way to act on resentment is to tell the person who is treating you unfairly that their behavior is not OK, and then to set some rules and boundaries. Since resentment takes time to build, it can be really easy to think it's too late to do anything. But don't worry – it's never too late to set a boundary. All you have to do is start a sentence with:

- *'Do you remember the conversation we had last week . . .'*

- *'Can I talk to you about something you said yesterday?'*

- *'Something that happened last month doesn't sit well with me and I want to discuss it with you.'*

Anger and resentment appear to try to tell you something. We have to pay attention to when something makes us uncomfortable and understand that the only reason that anger and resentment create discomfort within us is because we are not listening to these emotions. Then you need to act on this discomfort. You can't control what other people do, but you *can* control what you tolerate and how you react.

What are your boundaries?

You deserve to set the rules for your own life! Even if other people don't understand, it's up to you to decide what makes you uncomfortable and the rules that you want to set. You are prioritizing your comfort!

We need to start by figuring out how you feel and what you want to say 'no' to. Here are some of my examples, then you can think of some of your own:

It makes me uncomfortable when . . .
my friends tell other people my secrets.

It makes me uncomfortable when . . .
people make comments about my body.

It makes me uncomfortable when . . .
people come into my space without permission.

Your turn! Go back through the book and look at all the different types of boundaries we've discussed. By reflecting on the things that make you uncomfortable, you can now identify where you need to start setting more boundaries. Once you've figured out something that you don't like people doing, you then find the opposite of that so you can tell them what you DO want. For example, you could say:

'It makes me uncomfortable when you tell other people my secrets. If you want me to continue telling you my secrets, then you need to keep them between me and you and ask permission if you want to share them.'

If you are struggling to come up with your own list, recall times in the past where you have felt angry or resentful to get you started.

You know how maps give you directions on where to go next? Boundaries are the map telling the people in your life what they can be doing next to make you feel more comfortable!

No more people-pleasing pushovers, please

'No' is enough. Just that one word is enough. It's the equivalent to you putting your hand up and saying stop. And I get it – it seems like an impossible word to say, so what you might be tempted to do is . . .

waffle and . . .

waffle and . . .

waffle on.

- **NO MORE!**

- **No more justifying!**

- **No more over-explaining!**

- **No more apologizing!**

- **If your boundary has the word 'sorry' in it, you are doing it wrong.**

- **If your boundary is more than a few sentences, you are saying more than is necessary.**

Less is best. When you have a long, waffly paragraph explaining every single reason why your boundary is necessary, first of all, people get lost. They forget the original point you were making. Second, you turn your decision into a discussion, and your boundaries are **NOT** up for discussion.

Another reason you don't have to give reasons for your boundary is that you are giving that person a problem to solve. Let's say you're invited somewhere you don't want to go to, and so you make up the excuse that your parents say no. Your friend might offer to speak to your parents for you and, well, then you've stuck your foot in it, haven't you? Also, it gives your parents a bad reputation; they already have to say no in their own lives and it's not fair to blame them every time you are too scared to say no to your own friends. You wouldn't want them using you as their excuse either!

Instead, I would always recommend you speak the truth and say the bare minimum. Then the other person has a chance to speak, and if you need to say more after that, then say more.

Although 'no' is enough on its own, I know it's not always easy to say. But there are so many other ways to decline, object and refuse, so this section gives you all of those options. Here's a bunch of my favourites:

- **That isn't going to work for me.**

- **That's none of my business.**

- I'm fully booked at the moment.

- I won't be treated this way.

- That's not my thing.

- I am unable to.

- I need you to stop speaking to me like that.

- I'm not in the mood.

- That isn't my job.

- That doesn't concern me.

- I need you to stop.

- That makes me uncomfortable.

- I am unavailable.

- I don't have capacity for that.

The options are endless!

Someone might tell you that you're being really direct if you say these things. But what I've come to realize is: that doesn't matter! You can and should be direct, firm and confident with your boundaries. If you worry too much, you will end up tiptoeing around your boundaries, and that's what people-pleasers do. If you don't want to be a people-pleaser anymore, you have to stop thinking about them so much and start thinking about you. I want you to come up with a persona right here, right now. Someone who doesn't hold back when they're setting boundaries and is firm and fair with how they set them.

Give them a name . . .

When I was younger, I used to be called **Ms Sassy**. I spent a lot of time in hospital as a child, and even then, I had no issue telling everyone what I wanted and when I wanted it. As a result, all the nurses would call me Ms Sassy. Could Michelle sometimes be a pushover? Yes, occasionally. Was Ms Sassy a pushover? Never! So I channelled Ms Sassy and this helped me feel more confident about setting boundaries.Sometimes I still tap into Ms Sassy. She lives within me and allows me to be the most confident, powerful version of me.

Some of my followers even have a tactic of asking themselves, 'What would Michelle do?' When they want to set their boundaries, they remember my advice and if they have followed me long enough, they hear my voice in their head telling them how to set the boundary in the same way I would! Recall a person in your own life who doesn't tiptoe around people, trying to get others to like them, and ask yourself, 'What would they do?' Then do as they would. They would put themselves before other people because they are brave enough to be disliked. The difference is, they are able to say the sentence:

'It's OK if you don't like me.'

They aren't trying to change anyone else's opinion about them because they know they are allowed to set fair and firm boundaries.

How your boundary is received doesn't determine its success or failure. How you feel afterwards is what determines that. So stop focusing on people liking you, and instead focus on how proud you are of yourself when you set that boundary. Focus on the amazing sense of relief that you get when you've said no to something you don't appreciate. Focus on that feeling. Soak in it and let yourself absorb all the good feelings that come with it. It's pretty unforgettable. Then the next time you are scared to set a boundary, or scared that someone is going to think you are rude for doing so, just remember that feeling and realize *this* is what you are setting the boundary for. That's the reward for braving the tough moment!

It wouldn't be fair for me to assume that everyone likes being direct, though! I understand that everyone is different, and some people are naturally softer-spoken and prefer to be less blunt. I'll give you some gentler other options too, so everyone has a chance to start their journey towards setting healthy boundaries. But I should warn you now that you could be the politest person in the entire world and people still might find your boundary-setting rude. It isn't because you are actually rude – it's because your boundary is inconvenient or unfamiliar to them. Don't let this stop you from saying what you need.

The best way to soften a boundary is to put the emphasis of the sentence on a positive sentiment. You can do this by putting 'but' before the positive part. 'But' is what we call a nullifier, which means anything that comes before it is forgotten. It works like an eraser. So the person you are saying no to will hear the positive part of what you are saying, and you end the conversation on a happier note:

When declining an event . . .

'I am unable to come but have the best time! Can't wait to hear all about it!'

A teacher asks you to help out after school . . .

'I am unavailable but hope you find someone else to help you!'

A friend asks you to do their share of the group project . . .

'I won't be doing that, but I believe in you! You've got this!'

Your sibling is running late and wants you to wait . . .

'That doesn't work for me, but I'll go first and meet you there!'

Your parents want you to keep doing piano lessons . . .

'It doesn't make me happy but I would love to try another instrument.'

You now have a whole handbook of phrases and responses to try out and find out which ones work for you. You may want to personalize them and come up with your own language that sounds more like you. And you can even create a whole notebook of your own phrases. I love keeping these phrases handy in my notes section of my phone as a reminder of what I can say if I ever need to fire off a quick message saying no to someone. I also love to take screenshots of previous conversations so that when my brain tells me that I can't do it, have visual reminders of all the times I have succeeded in the past.

No means no

What do you do when you've said no to someone and they aren't listening, and they carry on doing what they want to do anyway? This is the part where I will show you how to stand up for yourself, reinforce your no, stay strong and hold your boundary firm. When you first start setting boundaries, some people might be a little shocked, so give them some time to adjust to the new you. As they adjust, all you need to do is be consistent. If they pretend you never set that boundary, you need to repeat yourself. If they walk all over the boundary you just set, you need to reinforce it, because you are not changing your mind.

I know when you set a boundary it's tempting to think 'Phew, glad that's over with!' Then the idea that you have to do it all over again is tiring. But if you quit now, then the energy you used the first time won't have been worth it. You have to do it over and over again throughout your life, and I promise it will get easier over time. Soon it will be so natural that it takes no energy at all because it becomes instinctive and the only way you know how to be. For now, it might be exhausting, but having no boundaries and never saying no is MORE exhausting. Boundaries are like brushing your teeth. Just because you set them yesterday doesn't mean you shouldn't set them today.

Other people might need time to learn that you are being serious, and the only way they realize this is if you continue to respond in the same way, no matter how they behave. You have to stay consistent! Their behaviour doesn't determine yours. **You choose your behaviour.** No matter how convincing they get, I want you to remember that your needs are important, and you can do this! You need to flex that boundary muscle and be confident, calm, cool and collected with your words so that everyone knows your boundaries are not to be messed with. Once they realize you mean business, you might be surprised that your boundaries go down a LOT more easily than expected! Here are some more handy phrases to reinforce your boundaries:

- *'I already said no and I need you to respect that.'*

- *'You know the boundary we spoke about yesterday? You are crossing that boundary again.'*

- *'This is the second time I am telling you to stop. Please listen to me.'*

- *'If you are expecting me to change my mind, I won't. I meant what I said.'*

- *'Did you hear what I just said to you? Great, because I need you to respect my decisions.'*

- *'I am going to need you to listen to my first "no". I am not going to repeat myself again.'*

- *'You are allowed to think that and I'm not changing my mind.g.'*

If they continue to ignore your boundaries, then it's consequence time. There has to be a consequence to breaking your boundaries repeatedly, otherwise the person breaking them might never stop. The biggest key to this is to set a consequence that you know you can follow through on. There is no point saying you are going to end the friendship if you know you aren't going to. The consequence needs to be something you can actually put in place, so here are some examples:

If someone raises their voice at you:

'If you continue speaking to me that way, I'm going to leave the room and you can find me when you are ready to speak to me at a normal volume.'

If someone keeps being mean about your friend:

'If you keep gossiping about my friend to me, I will tell them what you are saying.'

If someone is copying your work:

'If you keep copying my work, I will tell the teacher what you are doing.'

If they still don't respect your consequences, particularly in the last example, you can go to a trusted adult who makes you feel safe and tell them what's going on. It's so important to know how to say no on your own, but sometimes we all need a little help.

Another consequence of someone repeatedly breaking your boundaries might be distancing yourself from them for a while. This means spending less time with the person and maybe only spending the necessary time with them. For example, if you are in the same class, you still have to see them but you don't need to hang out with them after school anymore. You can also be more selective about the information they have access to.

I can't pretend that this is an easy thing to do. If it drives a wedge between you and a friend, this can be painful and it can become really hard to be around them.

But remember that you've got your invisible bubble protecting you. If they say unkind things in response, you can imagine that the mean words they throw at you are like arrows that bounce off the bubble.

In some cases, if someone's behaviour is making you unhappy or angry or uncomfortable, and they aren't respecting your no, you might want to end the friendship. You have the power to tell them that you don't want them in your life anymore.

Sometimes best friends aren't forever. Often a new, loyal friend is better than an old friend who is mistreating you. And friendships can change. Throughout your life, both in school and adulthood, you will lose friends and some friendships will end in heartbreak. It doesn't mean you are a bad friend; it doesn't even mean they are a bad friend. It just means that people change and as you change, you might want to change the people you have in your life – and you are allowed to do that! Regardless of who comes in and out of your life, you have to stick to your no.

No looks good on you!

Boundaries are a two-way street, which means other people have boundaries too! And it's just as important that we respect theirs. Yes, it can be inconvenient when someone sets boundaries with us, but it's a huge sign of respect! It means they trust us enough to speak honestly about how they are feeling, and they know our friendship is solid enough to be able to withstand some truth serum. It also means they trust us enough to tell us when we have done something wrong, rather than assuming we know or making us guess. And best of all, they are giving us a chance to act differently. Boundaries mean they know we have good intentions, are good people and they want us in their life – they just need to see a small change so we can both be happy! Before I knew all that I know now about boundaries, I used to think that when someone said no to me, it meant they were angry at me. But now I know the truth.

When you set boundaries with someone else, it's because **YOU** want a certain standard of behaviour. It's about what **YOU** want in your life and how **YOU** are feeling. That means that when someone else sets boundaries, they are doing this because of **THEIR** feelings and what **THEY** want. Just like your boundaries are not about them, their boundaries are not about you.

Sometimes when someone sets a new rule with you, it's the first time you've known about their boundary. How can you know if you cross someone's boundary if you didn't know it existed in the first place? The truth is you can't. But just because you did something wrong doesn't mean you are a bad person. It just means you are human! And now you know better, you can do better! Once someone tells you their boundary, you know what you need to do to change and improve your relationship. Reply to their boundary how you would want people to respond to yours: 'No worries, thanks for letting me know!' Or: 'I really appreciate you telling me; it won't happen again.'

Respecting their boundary means doing what they're asking even when you don't want to. Even when you know that if you keep pestering them, they will cave. Even when you think a little nudge might make them do what you want. So when your friend says no to going to a party, no more begging them to come out with you. When your mum says no you can't go to that sleepover, it's a no. We are going to get good at accepting other people's first no!

Because figuring out your relationship with the word 'no' isn't just about saying no – it's also about listening when other people say no. If you want your no to be respected, then the change starts with you.

Ten rules for starting your no journey

1. **You can't be liked by everyone**

2. **Listen to your anger and resentment to know if your boundary has been crossed**

3. **When someone sets a boundary with you, respect it**

4. **If you have an issue with someone, talk to them directly**

5. **You can't control someone's opinion of you**

6. **When setting boundaries, less is best**

7. **Your no is enough**

8. **How you feel is important, even if no one understands**

9. **Stay consistent with your no**

10. **Start saying no today**

A final word from me (and it's not NO!)

I know we have squeezed a lot into this book and I totally get it if you are feeling overwhelmed. 'No' might be one of the shortest words in the English language, but it can be scary to begin using it. What's the best way to get started? First, it's about coming to terms with your feelings and working out what makes you angry or resentful. Then, it's about exploring why certain things are making you uncomfortable and whether you could set a boundary to address that.

Next, choose your moment when you want to say no and actually say it! The end goal is for you to say no when you mean no, and to say yes when you mean yes. And to stick to your no.

Some people find it easier to start with a stranger and some people find it easier to start with someone close to them. If you want to start with a stranger, you could try it in a restaurant. restaurant. If a waiter asks you if you like something and you don't - let them know. You could also try it in school. So when a teacher asks if you understand something, and you don't, then actually say no. If you want to start with your nearest and dearest, then the next time your best friend asks you for a favour and you aren't in the mood, it's time to tell them no.

The more you experiment with it, the more you will realize the power that 'no' unleashes. It makes you more confident. It helps you understand yourself better. And it helps you honour what you need in order to be happy and comfortable.

If this journey feels daunting and scary, share all the secrets in this book with your friends. You can make it into a fun game where you do a happy dance every time one of you says no. Even now, my friends are my biggest boundary cheerleaders! They want me to be as powerful as I can be and they know boundaries are what give me (and everyone else!) power.

Most of all, I want you to know and believe deep in your heart that you deserve to set boundaries. As you get older, you might find you have new people you are going to have to learn to say no to, such as bosses and housemates or even roommates! You are learning a skill that will last a lifetime. You are well ahead of the curve!

You are allowed to say no! And you don't need to say yes to every request and demand made of you in order to be a good person. You are good enough just as you are, and your no is an important part of who you are. It's time to embrace your no and get started!

You've got this!

Acknowledgements

When I was still a child and adults asked me what I wanted to do for a job, my answer would often change from being a mum, to a teacher and then, at eleven years old, I made my mind up and eventually decided on becoming a psychologist (which never happened!). But long before I knew which career I wanted, there was one thing I always knew I was certain of: I wanted to work with children. Even though I was still a child myself! I started working in schools when I was a teenager, but somehow life worked out in a way where that pipe dream never happened. So this book has given me a little piece of that back and has filled my heart in a way I can't even describe! It is proof that you should never give up on a dream. Just because it hasn't been achieved now, it just means it hasn't been achieved yet!

Being a newbie children's author means a number of people had to take a chance on me, so I couldn't end the book without a whole bunch of thank yous.

Thank you so much to Chloe Seager and the whole Madeleine Milburn team. It's hard to believe that the book came out of asking you one question: Everyone keeps asking me to write a children's book on boundaries, do you think that idea has potential? Turns out it did! And it's been so fulfilling trying something new and getting out of my comfort zone! Thank you for all your support along the way, and I have loved working together!

Thank you so much to my brilliant editor, Phoebe Jascourt, and the whole Puffin team. From the very beginning, you've been as passionate about this book as I was. I love that you've been such a champion for boundaries and you made all of this possible by doing all the work behind the scenes to convince everyone that this was a needed book.

Thank you so much to all the wonderful women at Belle PR. You are all the best cheerleaders, and it means the world to have you lifting up my voice. I am so grateful to have you all in my corner and couldn't do it without all your encouragement and empowering me to be bigger, braver and louder!

And finally, to every kid out there who feels lost or doesn't know who they are yet – you aren't meant to. Life is all about figuring out stuff as you go and it's a good thing, because that means you have more surprises to come. Now I look back and want to give a shout-out to little me because she weathered teachers calling her too bossy and too loud, and braved some really rubbish moments to become the person writing this book today. I couldn't be who I am without her. My childhood wasn't the easiest, and if you are going through the tough stuff right now, please know it gets better and you are never alone. Someone loves you, and sometimes that's easy to forget, but I wish I knew back then that talking to someone always helps. One day, you are going to look back on all of this and wonder how you were ever scared to say no ... I know I do!

Index